vietnamstyle

Photographs by **Luca Invernizzi Tettoni**

Bertrand de Hartingh and **Anna Craven-Smith-Milnes**

PERIPLUS EDITIONS
Singapore • Hong Kong • Indonesia

Published by Periplus Editions (HK) Ltd, with editorial offices at 130 Joo Seng Road, #06-01 Singapore 368357.

Copyright © 2007 Periplus Editions (HK) Ltd
Photographs © 2007 Luca Invernizzi Tettoni

ISBN 13 978 0 7946 0018 1
ISBN 10 0 7946 0018 2
Distributed by:

Asia Pacific
Berkeley Books Pte Ltd, 130 Joo Seng Road #06-01,
Singapore 368357.
Tel: (65) 6280 1330; Fax: (65) 6280 6290
E-mail: inquiries@periplus.com.sg
http://www.periplus.com

North America, Latin America and Europe
Tuttle Publishing, 364 Innovation Drive, North Clarendon,
Vermont 05759, USA.
Tel: (802) 773 8930; Fax: (802) 773 6993
E-mail: info@tuttlepublishing.com
http://www.tuttlepublishing.com

Japan
Tuttle Publishing, Yaekari Building, 3F, 5-4-12 Osaki,
Shinagawa-ku, Tokyo 141-0032.
Tel: (81) 3 5437 0171; Fax: (81) 3 5437 0755
E-mail: tuttle-sales@gol.com

First edition
10 09 08 07
5 4 3 2 1

Printed in Singapore

Endpapers: Murals at Cao Dai Temple, Tay Ninh, representing celestial heavens (page 98).
Page 1: Propaganda art on glassware at Saigon Kitsch, Ho Chi Minh City (page 206).
Page 2: Joss sticks in front of a bamboo curtain.
Pages 4–5: High ogival vaults supported by columns separate the sitting room in the main part of the original Loan de Leo Foster House from the dining room and a small bedroom (page 86).
Page 6: View over Truc Back Lake, Hanoi, at dusk, taken from the top of the Sofitel Metropole Hanoi (page 116).

CONTENTS

VERNACULAR STYLES

THE LAND OF THE RISING DRAGON

Hanoi, Saigon, Hue, ... the names conjure up images of the Far East, of glorious and mysterious emperors, incense floating around wooden pillars in pagodas, golden and red boats slowly sailing up rivers, carved stones of old temples. French cities in a faraway world, Citroens and cyclos trailing in crowded streets, people dressed in colorful clothes or white suits sipping coffee along boulevards planted with trees, umbrellas à la Manet on the Mekong. Soldiers dying in the mud, helicopters flying over desperate civilians, silent guerrillas dressed in black, lines of armored vehicles devastating paddy fields. Dien Bien Phu and Khe Sanh, Ho Chi Minh, heat and blood, napalm and agent orange, colors spread along pages in magazines once read by millions anxious to know about "Nam."

These images, true or false, have shaped the collective imagination about Vietnam. But those who have been there know that the country is much more. Far from being devastated, in reality Vietnam is filled with dazzling natural beauty, a verdant tapestry of soaring mountains, fertile alluvial deltas, primeval rainforests, mysterious caves, fascinating rock formations, sinuous rivers, spectacular beaches and alluring islands, complemented by peaceful villages, ancient historic sites and pulsating cities, and populated by an incredibly resilient people! In a remarkably short time – just over two decades – since the North and South were reunited in 1975, Vietnam has been able to offer visitors a feast of culture and history – not to mention probably the best cuisine in Asia! In the north, alpine peaks, the Red River delta, the Cao Bang and Vinh Ven plains, Halong Bay, historic Hanoi and a diversity of ethnolinguistic minorities attract visitors. In the center, the ancient imperial city of Hue, the many ethnic minorities and the beaches, dunes and lagoons have tourist pull. In the south, Ho Chi Minh city – the former Saigon – offers a modern experience while the Mekong delta to the south provides a fascinating insight into life on a flood plain.

Against this complex topographical background, Vietnam's history, both early and recent, has been characterized by a permanent flux of migrations, internal movements and an almost continuous struggle for independence. For centuries Vietnam fought to maintain its identity: against China that, for nearly 1,000 years, put the country under a domination that was thrown off in the ninth century, and never ceased to pretend to be the legitimate ruler of its southern neighbour (hence the name of the country, "beyond the South"); against France, whose colonization lasted less then a century but deeply transformed the country before its rule was ended at Dien Bien Phu; against the USA, that launched a vain but devastating war until the fall of Saigon allowed Vietnam to enjoy peace and started the economic process that make it today one of the fastest growing emerging countries. Thus

Right Peaceful hamlets, verdant paddy fields dotted with tomb-stones and tranquil waterways contribute to the quiet charm of North Vietnam.

Vietnam learned to live by many standards and develop a superb ability to syncretize its would-be masters' cultural patterns into its own culture.

The multiplicity of Vietnam's early and recent history is evident throughout its culture, including its spiritual life and architecture, which are often inextricably mixed. Spiritual life in Vietnam comprises a medley of belief systems, including Buddhism (the dominant religion), Christianity and the curious fruits that sometimes developed from these faiths crossing, such as Caodism. Architecturally, there is a hodgepodge of styles although most constructions fall into five main categories: Vietnamese vernacular, ethnic vernacular, traditional Chinese, French colonial and Vietnamese modern.

Single-story vernacular Vietnamese buildings, commonly seen all over the country but particularly in the villages and hamlets around Hanoi, are distinctive for their wooden framework, put together by shafts, dowels or wooden pegs, heavy flat-tiled roofs designed to withstand typhoons, brick, bamboo, wood or bast fiber mat walls and packed earth or tile floors. None have ceilings or chimneys. (It is not uncommon to find Hanoi residents purchasing such houses for amalgamation with their existing homes.) Larger traditional community halls or *dinh*, usually built on sturdy piles, are also of wooden construction.

Ethnic vernacular buildings, whether raised on piles or built flat on the ground, remain in mountainous areas, midlands, and plains throughout the country where they are built of lightweight materials to enable disassembly and reassembly as the need arises. The recent permanent settlement of villages, however, has resulted in the adoption of more durable designs. Timber is increasingly used as the walls are load-bearing and roofs may be made with tiles or zinc, a popular material since it displays the wealth of the homeowner. Painted window frames, doors or pediments, unknown in transportable houses, are now worth the time and money spent on them.

The Chinese influence on Vietnamese architecture is most obvious in the country's vast numbers of historic temples and monastries, especially its pagodas, whose distinctive features include roofs with elevated hip rafters and half-round tiles, heavy ornamentation and the lavish use of embellishments and motifs. Although the layout and orientation and the use of statuary and steles and other exterior elements are usually Chinese in origin, the architectural details of Vietnamese pagodas, although superficially similar to their Chinese antecedents, differ greatly. Chinese influence is also seen clearly in the architecture and furnishings of the the long, thin "tube" townhouses of Hanoi and Hoi An.

Colonial buildings in Vietnam are more than a direct replica of French architecture. Adaptation to a very different climate led to many distinctive features, making the style into a genre in its own right. Good examples of colonial buildings can be found all over the country, but the Town Hall in Ho Chi Minh City and the Opera House in Hanoi, along with the city's many colonial villas, are particularly splendid examples.

Whereas heavy taxes on the frontage of old vernacular townhouses led to the advent of "tube" houses in Hanoi and Hoi An, spiralling land values have placed a premium on height. Today, in and around Vietnam's cities, traditional single-story homes vie for attention with a new architectural genre – narrow houses on tiny patches of land, often rising several stories high and displaying a strange pastiche of French architecture – ornate balconies, cupolas, decorations fashioned in cement and painted in pastel shades.

the citadel at hue

HUE IS A UNIQUE CITY that is unmatched in Indochina. It has everything to please the most demanding visitor, from royal palaces and mausoleums to old residential areas, both Vietnamese and French. The Perfume River offers a constantly changing landscape, while everyday life takes place on its sampans. As the capital of Vietnamese Buddhism, Hue has more temples than any other town in Vietnam; these, along with its garden houses, contribute to its considerable charm.

It also has an extremely serene atmosphere, probably because the city is strictly laid out according to *phuong thuy* or geomancy rules. One of these rules calls for the respect of geological veins or lines, the main ones being likened to the bodies of the dragon and the tiger. Geomancy thus organizes architecture and urbanism in respect to these veins. The core of Hue city, the Imperial City, is precisely situated at the crossroads of two axes, thus allowing the "White Tiger to be seated" and the "Azure Dragon to curl up." From the main esplanade in front of the Supreme Concord Palace starts a northwest to southeast oriented axis. It links the palace with Ngo Môn Gate, then Ngu Binh Hill (which acts likes a natural screen protecting the city from evil influences) and, 43 miles (70 km) away, with Nui Ke sacred mountain. There, the emperor performed an annual sacrifice to the gods to ensure the fertility of the land, the source of all wealth. The other axis follows the river's route up to Con Da Vien and Con Hen islands.

Although the city was first created as a Cham outpost at the beginning of our era, Hue rose to prominence when, under the name of Phu Xuan, it became the capital of the Nguyen lords in 1687. When Gia Long, the heir of the Nguyen lords, defeated all his foes and created the Nguyen Dynasty in 1802, he quite naturally decided to establish his capital in his ancestors' main town. It was renamed Hue. The city remained the capital until 1945 when the Democratic Republic of Vietnam chose to move the capital back to Hanoi. Although fierce combat during the war severely damaged the Citadel, massive restoration projects under the auspices of UNESCO are improving matters. Recognized in 1993 as a "Heritage of Humanity" site, the Citadel and its mausoleums are slowly regaining their original magnificence.

Hue's Citadel (Kinh Thanh) is the only extant citadel in Indochina. Erected between 1804 and 1819, it was admired by foreign visitors from the first days of its completion. It is certainly an impressive sight, if only for its 6 mile (10 km) long, 66 ft (20 m) wide and 23 ft (7 m) high surrounding stone walls, which are punctuated by ten gates.

Right The Ngo Môn Gate (Moon Gate) is the most impressive of the four main gates piercing the 6 mile (10 km) defensive wall of the moated Citadel. Today, it is the main entrance for visitors into the city. In Imperial times, only the emperor was permitted to enter through its central doors. On top of the gate is the Ngu Phung, the Belvedere of the Five Phoenixes, where the emperor would appear during ceremonies. The tiles in the center of the roof are in imperial yellow, while the roofs to either side are green.

Left The other three main gates leading into the Citadel are simpler two-story stone structures, each symbolizing the characteristic of a human being. The East Gate shown here is known as the Gate of Humanity.

Within these walls stands the Imperial City (Hoang Thanh), with its administrative buildings and high-ranking civil servants' houses. A second enclosure is devoted to the palaces and temples that made up the Forbidden City (Tu Cam Thanh or Purple City), where the emperor and his family lived. That part of the Citadel was almost entirely destroyed in 1968 during the Tet offensive, although some of its buildings have since been restored.

Except for the outside walls and gates, the Citadel is made entirely of wood and tiles. The styles of the various buildings are distinctive, each being constructed according to its function, although at first glance they look the same as any other wooden Vietnamese buildings. Religious buildings have a relatively low, rectangular shape, and thus look more like long galleries than Buddhist or Taoist temples. The administrative buildings, including the Throne Hall, are higher and squarer, a design rarely employed in traditional Vietnamese architecture. Domestic buildings, such as pavilions, are either built in the French style, having been constructed under French rule, or are more impressive one- or two-story houses designed according to the tastes and ideas of the emperors responsible for their construction. While the Forbidden City was painted in yellow, the color reserved for the emperor, most of the Imperial City's buildings are decorated in red. This is considered the most auspicious color in Vietnamese tradition.

Today, one enters the Citadel through the North Gate (Ngo Môn), which is actually in the south since it led to the north and stands behind the Flag Tower. Built in 1836 by King Minh Mang, the North Gate gives access to the Imperial City. Only the emperor was allowed to enter through its central doors, which led to a bridge across a lotus pond. Mandarins and visitors were required to go through the lateral doors and around the pond. The Five-Phoenix Belvedere also had restricted access. It was here that the emperor addressed the court and watched feasts and parades. This is where the last emperor, Bao Dai, abdicated on August 30, 1945. The South Gate is the most sophisticated of the four main Citadel gates, while the other three are simpler two-story stone structures that were used on less important occasions. Since the Nguyen Dynasty strictly followed Confucian rules, the three simpler gates symbolized the characteristic of a human being, the East Gate being the Humanity Gate, the West Gate the Virtue Gate, and the South Gate the Peace Gate. The bridge over the pond leads to the Bai Dinh esplanade, used by mandarins during major ceremonies held in the main building of the Imperial City, the Thai Hoa Palace or Palace of the Supreme Concord. Erected in 1803, then moved to its current position in 1833, the palace houses the Throne Hall, distinguished by its eighty red-and-gold lacquered columns. It was here that the emperor held official audiences. The Left (Huu) and Right (Ta) Service pavilions, where civilian and military mandarins respectively worked, flank the palace. From the Throne Hall and through the Golden Gate (Dai Cung), the emperor and his eunuchs could enter the Forbidden City.

In the west of the Imperial City stand several buildings of great spiritual importance. The three-story Hien Lam Pavilion (Glory Pavilion) is the highest building in the Citadel. Built in 1821, it is part of a complex of three temples devoted to the Nguyen Dynasty official cult, and is probably the most elegant structure of the entire Citadel. It was built in honor of those who had helped the Nguyen to establish their dynasty, which explains why it stands in front of the Dynastic Temple (Thê Mieu) dedicated to ten Nguyen emperors, from Gia Long to Khai Dinh, the father of the last emperor. Also built in 1821, this temple houses a wooden lacquered altar for each emperor: on each stands his portrait and the usual liturgical objects: incense burner, vase and candlestick. Since women could not enter this temple, another dynastic temple was specially built for them.

Just behind stands the Queen Mother's Palace, an interesting mix of traditional and colonial styles. It is almost the only palace that is furnished. There is a typical French sitting room suite and a more traditional chest of drawers set in the middle of columns ornamented with calligraphic panels. It provides some idea of life in such palaces, as does the nearby Longevity Temple, which was used as a place of relaxation by the emperors. In addition to beautiful carved lacquered panels, it is noteworthy for its colored windows that offer a refreshing contrast to the omnipresent wood, stones and bricks found elsewhere.

Right The main building of the Citadel, the Thai Hoa Palace, houses the magnificent Throne Hall, where the emperor would meet foreign rulers and emissaries, high-ranking ministers and other dignitaries. Recent renovation work has restored its lacquer and gilt interior to its former glory.

Left The Throne Hall stands in the Great Rites Courtyard. The steles on each side of the courtyard indicate the designated area for mandarins and court officials.

Right Huge ornate pillars and stone dragons distinguish the back of the Throne Hall, which leads to a courtyard which was once the entrance to the Forbidden Purple City. As with the rest of the palace complex, the Throne Hall was badly damaged during shelling by American warships in 1968 and remained in a state of disrepair until recently.

Far left The Bridge of Golden Waters, which only the emperor was allowed to cross, leads between two tranquil, lotus-filled ponds to the Thai Hoa Palace. The yellow-tiled roof of the palace is supported by eighty massive wooden columns lacquered a deep red and decorated with golden dragons, the emblem of the Nguyen Dynasty.

Right This solitary, intricately wrought golden throne served as the emperor's seat in the Throne Hall. It was used during official ceremonies and important court proceedings. On these occasions the emperor would wear a crown decorated with the Nine Dragons design, a golden robe and a jade belt, and would hold in his hands incense sticks or cinnamon bars.

19

Above The elegant three-story Hien Lam, Pavilion of the Glorious Coming, at 82 ft (25 m) high is the tallest building in the imperial enclosure. It was constructed in 1821 by Emperor Ming Mang and dedicated to the Nguyen Dynasty. The nine dynastic bronze urns standing at the entrance to the temple, each dedicated to one of the Nguyen emperors, were cast in the 1830s, and are embellished with bas-reliefs of symbolic creatures and plants.

Right Located in the southwest of the Imperial City, the Dynastic Temple (Thê Mieu), dedicated to ten Nguyen emperors, houses a wooden lacquered funerary altar for each emperor, bearing portraits and various liturgical objects.

Right The ceiling of the Dynastic Temple, one of the few buildings spared destruction during the American War, can be seen today in all its original splendor.

Right The ceiling of the Dynastic Temple, one of the few buildings spared destruction during the American War, can be seen today in all its original splendor.

Left In addition to the main entrance gate, the Citadel has three simpler gates built in stone which were used on less important occasions. Each symbolized the characteristics of the human being. The West Gate shown here is known as the Virtue Gate.

Below This photograph of "A young prince and his porters and escort at Hue" attests to the rich cultural lifestyle enjoyed by members of the royal family and to the large numbers of people – mandarins, court officers, civil servants, consorts, concubines, retainers and others – who worked and lived within the three concentric enclosures of the 1330 acre (520 hectare) Citadel.

Above right Although the drawing room in the Queen Mother's residence is built in Vietnamese style, most of the furnishungs were imported from the West.

Below right The residence of the Queen Mother comprises some buildings inspired by French colonial architecture and others in Vietnamese style.

royal mausoleums of hue

HUE'S MAUSOLEUMS were constructed following the same *phuong thuy* (geomancy) principles that dictated the layout of the Imperial City. Located along the Perfume River, west of the Citadel, their sites and designs were chosen with great care, since they would become the permanent residences for the remains of the deceased emperors. The same attention was paid to their construction, so much so that they very often became the emperors' favorite "country retreats."

All the mausoleums follow the same basic plan: a huge honor courtyard opens onto an alley bordered by stone statues of the emperor's highest military and civilian mandarins. This leads, sometimes through a wooden gate, to the main pavilion. There stands the emperor's main altar, with a stele recounting his virtues. Around this pavilion other buildings are usually devoted to his wives and concubines. A bit further away stands the emperor's temple, with its main altar and often with his favorite objects. The last building of the compound is the grave itself, which is always closed.

Since the emperors personally supervised the construction of their own mausoleums, these usually reflect the period in which they lived as well as their individual personalities. The mausoleum of Gia Long (r. 1804–20), for instance, is sober, almost savage. In contrast, Gia's son Minh Mang (r. 1820–41), who designed and built his own mausoleum during the first three years of the reign of his son and successor Thieu Tri (r. 1841–7), is more elaborate. The plan of Gia Long's mausoleum is inspired by the figure three. Three granite staircases lead to the stele pavilion, which is accessed by a beautiful row of red doors. From there, three terraces open to the Sung An temple. Three bridges then cross the Pure Clarity pond to reach the Minh Lau pavilion, which dominates three esplanades that symbolize heaven, earth and water.

The mausoleum of Tu Duc (r. 1847–83) is without any doubt the most beautiful and sophisticated of all the mausoleums in Hue. This emperor, whose reign was the longest ever in Vietnamese history, was a poet and a man well versed in literature and the arts. The design of his mausoleum was more like a residence than a tomb and he used it as such during his long reign. Built by more than 3,000 men between 1864 and 1867, the mausoleum opens with the Vu Khiem gate. A paved alley leads to a water lily and lotus pond dominated by a wooden library where the emperor liked to write his poetry. From here, an imposing staircase leads to the Hoa Khiem temple, which houses the steles and thrones of the emperor and empress, as well as some of the emperor's

Page 25 Probably one of the most graceful of the eight Nguyen Dynasty tombs, this mausoleum was built to Emperor Minh Mang's own design after his death in 1841. The grounds are large and peaceful. The entrance is guarded by statues of civil and military officials and opens up to a courtyard with three main temples, including one dedicated to his empress.

Below Red lacquered doors pivot open into the main pavilion inside Minh Mang's mausoleum.

Right Minh Mang's interest in architecture introduced a lot of new construction to the Imperial City, mostly in the Chinese tradition, not only during his reign but also after the construction of the buildings in his mausoleum.

Below right A shrine dedicated to Minh Mang and his empress sits on top of an altar in the Minh Mang mausoleum.

personal objects, such as a candlestick presented by Emperor Napoleon III. The temple is ornamented with beautiful and extremely rare paintings on glass depicting famous scenes from Chinese literature and history. The temple overlooks the honor courtyard, which contains stone statues of elephants, horses and mandarins, and in turn leads to the stele pavilion. Tu Duc himself wrote the text on the carved stele. From the pavilion one can see the grave, which is said to be empty. Nobody knows exactly where the king's remains lie, as legend has it that the 200 servants who buried the king were executed soon after the burial.

The Khai Dinh mausoleum (r. 1916–25) is much more modern looking, since the emperor was fond of French architecture and design. A combination of classic Vietnamese style and French palace architecture, it was built between 1920 and 1931. Even though the staircases and temples are made of concrete, which does not make it the most beautiful building in Hue, it is heavily ornamented and is the only mausoleum with painted ceilings.

Left The Longevity Temple in the Imperial city was built in 1822 during the reign of Minh Mang.

Above right A small stained-glass window in the temple. Unusually, clear glass was also used in door panels.

Right The interaction between Oriental and Western styles can be seen in these very unusual beautiful wooden doors with stained-glass windows.

Above The tomb of the Emperor Tu Duc is one of the most elegant mausoleums in Hue and sits in a garden with a magnificent lake and pavilion complex. The Chinese-style pavilion was the centerpiece of the tomb, a place where the emperor could sit in peace and write his poetry.

Below left This extremely rare painting on glass shows a contemporary depiction of court life, in this case a feast. The emperor sits on a raised stage at one end while the guests, dressed in traditional costumes, sit at long tables set with many dishes. Musical ensembles provide entertainment.

Below right One of the statues guarding the mausoleum. The tombs of both high-ranking mandarins and emperors follow the Chinese tradition of being accessed by a grand alley flanked by stone images of soldiers and animals. The number of images depended on rank.

Right Minh Mang's tomb is built like a miniature palace set in gardens and surrounded by ponds and lakes. The Sung An temple shown here is dedicated to his empress. Vietnamese funerary architecture was strongly influenced by geomancy, with the sites and the size of buildings being determined by strict rules.

Left Emperor Khai Dinh's mausoleum was built during the 1920s, and in comparison to earlier tombs is a much more modern interpretation of both Oriental and Western architectural nuances. Most of the vast pillars and statues are built in concrete. In this first main courtyard, two rows of statues representing the emperor's soldiers and mandarins, flanked by life-sized elephants, face the court center.

Above The walls in the main room of the emperor's tomb are covered in an elaborate glass and porcelain design.

Right The ceiling clearly shows a mixture of Oriental and Western styles, with nine painted dragons dancing among gray clouds.

garden houses of hue

IN THE CITY OF HUE one finds a number of garden houses that date from the nineteenth century to the present day. Garden house architecture follows exactly the same principles as the imperial palaces of Hue. The house structure is basically a timber, load-bearing frame that can be easily dismantled. The wood used is not as precious as the *lim* (ironwood) reserved for temples and palaces, but tends to be any of the rot-resistant varieties such as *kien*, *mit* and *gu*. As in palace architecture, such houses respect the rules of geomancy (*phuong thuy*), with elements of the garden being used as natural screens. The ancestor's altar, the protective plant screen and an ornamental pond are usually aligned on the same axis. Sometimes, again respecting *phuong thuy* principles, the garden and house entrances are not on the same axis or, alternately, the plant screen may protect the main door of the house from any bad spirits tempted to enter. The garden is thus a part of the house. As well as having aesthetic and spiritual functions, it also ensures the rapid absorption of excess rainwater and keeps the temperature at an acceptable level during the hot Hue summers.

Most of Hue's extant garden houses have retained traditional styles and forms. However, many have incorporated French elements, such as a brick wall painted in yellow, blue or green, or floor tiles and furniture, resulting in a pleasant marriage between French classic shapes and Vietnamese traditional wood craftsmanship. Some are also relatively new, having been built only a few years ago and thus maintaining a lively tradition.

The Ngoc Son garden house, one of the oldest in Hue, is believed to have been built between 1885 and 1888. The Emperor Dong Khanh (who reigned only from 1885 to 1888 before the French deposed him) gave it to his daughter, the Princess Ngoc Son. Today, his direct descendant, Mr An, looks after the house. The house was built in traditional Vietnamese style according to strict rules of geomancy. The main entrance faces the garden, not the street, and a protective bamboo screen separates the main door of the house from the pond. Inside, the library has changed little during the last 100 years. The only traces of French influence are the blue wooden shutters on the doors and windows, which are usually kept open, but are closed when the midday sun is too bright.

The Y Thao garden-house is a good example of a recent development. Its owners, Mrs Cuc and Mr Hoa (in Vietnam, married women keep their maiden names) wanted to build a place to house their collections and to create a garden that testifies to their love of Hue's traditions. Their house, built on a 14,000 sq ft (1300 sq m) plot of land, is a harmonious mixture of Vietnamese and French traditions. Inside is a beautiful collection of Hue ceramics (Hue has been a ceramic and porcelain production center for centuries and its blue-and-white pieces are famous worldwide) and a number of traditional paintings, either on glass or silk or made of wooden panels inlaid with mother-of-pearl (an art still alive in Hue). Outside, the garden is a combination of seven different smaller gardens, which symbolize either famous mountains or the five notes of the Vietnamese musical scale.

The one-story An Hien house, built in the late 1880s, was the residence of Emperor Duc Duc's (Tu Duc's nephew) eighteenth daughter. Although it has changed hands several times, its traditional features have been retained. The river-facing entrance, with an arch topped by a tiger head and the Chinese characters for An Hien, resembles an old temple entrance. The main area of the house, devoted to the ancestor's altar, is divided into three parts. The living quarters, on each side of the altar, are small and are bare of furniture except for beds. The walls are made of wood, the only concession to contemporary needs being electricity and a few chairs. Most of the 43,800 sq ft (4068 sq m) plot is taken up by the garden, which has the most beautiful orchard in Hue.

Page 34 Garden houses are a unique feature of Hue and date from the beginning of the nineteenth century. The houses were usually privately owned and set in attractive formal gardens. Some have connections with the old Royal Imperial Court.

Page 35 Harmony between the city's ancient ambience and its poetic landscape is reflected in this small temple perched on the banks of the Perfume River.

Opposite The Ngoc Son garden house was built by Emperor Dong Khanh for his daughter Princess Ngoc Son. It is still occupied by one of his descendants.

Left The interior has changed little in a hundred years and is well preserved by its current owner, historian Phan Thuan An, the author of several books on the culture and architecture of Hue.

Below The house is divided into three bays. In the middle is An's impressive library and an altar dedicated to Buddha as well as to ancestor worship.

37

Above left and below The Y Thao house contains an impressive collection of antiques, including Hue blue-and-white ceramics, traditional glass and silk paintings and wooden panels inlaid with mother-of-pearl. The collection is laid out to delineate between pieces used by the imperial family and those used by the mandarins.

Above The large stone rocks in the garden symbolize the mountain ranges around Hue and act as a screen against the wind. Tropical plants, bonsai and small rockeries are all typical of Hue's garden houses.

Right Compared to many of the garden houses in Hue, the Y Thao house is comparatively modern and was built by its present owners as a place for their collection of antiques. The garden is a combination of seven small gardens, each symbolizing different characteristics of the Vietnamese countryside.

Above The entrance to the An Hien garden house is from the road which runs alongside the Perfume River. Through the archway, topped by a tiger's head and the name An Hien in Chinese characters, is a broad path leading visitors through the garden to the house.

Left Originally the residence of Emperor Duc Duc's eighteenth daughter, the one-story house was built around 1880 and is a classic example of traditional Vietnamese architecture. An expansive ceramic-tiled roof is supported by large wooden pillars with richly carved beams and doorways. The lily pond in front is to ward off bad spirits.

Right The main area inside the house is devoted to the ancestor's altar, while the rest of the interior is sparsely furnished. The ceramic-tiled floor is typical of this style of building in Hue. All the tiles, including the roof tiles, were manufactured locally.

Opposite Successive generations of the same family have lived in the Phung Hung house since it was first built in 1780. The ground floor was originally used for storage and has an opening in the ceiling to enable goods to be hoisted upstairs during floods. Flooding remains a problem for such merchant houses in Hue.

Left Traditional wooden furniture inlaid with mother-of-pearl was used to welcome traders to this merchant's home. The house is supported by eighty ironwood columns set in marble bases. All the materials used in the house's construction, including the wood and marble, were sourced locally and are still being used in today's buildings.

chinese houses of hoi an

FROM THE SIXTEENTH to the nineteenth centuries, the harbor town of Hoi An, not far from Danang, attracted merchants from all over Asia. Although they comprised mainly Japanese and Chinese, they also included Portuguese, Dutch, French and British. All came to trade in cinnamon, pepper, paper, ceramics, medicinal plants and, above all, the silk that was – and still is – the region's main glory.

Sailing requires good winds that are not always blowing at the right time, and trading companies like to have people they trust in harbors. Thus, foreign merchants began to settle in the city. Even if it never had more than a few hundred permanent residents, it often housed thousands of foreigners, especially Chinese and Japanese (until 1637), each living in their own areas, with their own rules. They built their own dwellings, temples and congregation halls. By the end of the sixteenth century, the town was split between a Chinese district and Japanese one.

The Chinese district, where scores of merchant houses have been preserved, is a must for any art and architecture lover. The ground floors of the long, thin houses were devoted to trading, while the second floors housed altars of the ancestors and Taoist deities – customarily just below the ceiling.

One particularly noteworthy example of a Hoi An merchant house is the Phung Hung house. Built in 1780, to date it has been inhabited by eight generations of the same family. The house has kept its original structure because it was built with fine materials and has been very well maintained over the years. Its eighty ironwood columns and their marble bases, all the wooden rafters and shutters, both interior and exterior balconies, and its *yin* and *yang* roof tiles are exactly as they were the year the house was built. The structure combines Chinese (architecture), Vietnamese (furniture) and Japanese (roof) design styles but is actually quite simple in layout and structure. The ground floor formerly stored merchandise, although a square opening in the ceiling allowed goods to be lifted upstairs during frequent flooding. A sitting room decked out with *gu* (wooden furniture inlaid with mother-of-pearl) welcomed fellow traders. Today, that sitting room, which dates from the nineteenth century, is on the second floor, as is the altar room, the most important space in the house.

Opposite the Phung Hung house stands a dwelling that offers a beautiful succession of rooms, the second one being topped by an opening in the roof allowing light to enter.

Most Hoi An houses have no openings other than on the façade and at the back. The Tran family house illustrates how such houses often had a primarily religious purpose. In 1802, Tran Tu Nhac, one of Emperor Gia Long's most trusted mandarins, was sent as a delegate to China. Before leaving, he built the house in order to thank his ancestors for their protection. Even though it has some rooms used by family and guests, its main *raison d'etre* is as the family cult place; this is illustrated by a red panel in front of the main altar, which reads Duong Tu Tran (Tran Temple). In the olden days, men were required to enter the house through the left doors on the façade, while women used the right. The central door is reserved for elders and is used during major festivals such as Tet (the New Year Festival). To enter the worshipping part of the house from the living quarters, one has to go under a timber beam, forcing people to bend their heads in a demonstration of respect. The clan's main altar displays the usual liturgical objects as well as small boxes, arranged by chronological and social order, in which are kept relics and a biography of each deceased clan member. These boxes are opened only during festivals. On each side two lanterns are a reminder that this is the Tran clan cult house.

In contrast, the Diep Dong Nguyen house has a more vernacular atmosphere. In 1856, Ye Hong Chun, a Chinese merchant, established a shop that traded in silk, commodities and other goods. In 1900 the shop and its façade were enlarged by Ye Jia Song (Diep Gia Tong in Vietnamese), the founder's fourth-generation nephew. It houses an impressive collection of around 1,000 ceramics and other Chinese antiques. In the second-floor yellow sitting room is a blue-and-white plate purchased by Emperor Khai Dinh. The house has two altars: the left is for the ancestors who lived in China, the right for more recent family members, whose portraits are displayed on the walls. The living quarters, a single room on the second floor, is decorated with colonial era lamps, wooden carved Vietnamese panels and *gu* furniture, while the library is mainly in the Chinese style.

Left The covered atrium at the center of the house is flooded with natural light and is decorated with traditional furniture and ceramics.

Above The sitting room on the second floor runs from the front to the back of the house, with a shuttered walkway around the central atrium. There are two altars in the room: one to the left of the picture behind a wooden column, and the other mounted high up on a wall in the center of the room.

Opposite The Tran family house was built as much to house a temple as a home. Erected in 1802 by a civil service mandarin, Tran Tu Nhuc, it contains two main areas: one for worship and the other for the family to reside in.

Left The sign above the family ancestral altar reads Tran Temple. Behind it, small boxes contain relics and a biography of the deceased.

Below Along the sitting room walls are three entrances with sliding doors: the left is for men to use, the right for women, while the central doorway is only opened on special occasions to welcome home dead ancestors.

Above The Diep Dong Nguyen house, built in the nineteenth century by a Chinese merchant, an ancestor of the present inhabitants, is beautifully preserved with an impressive collection of ceramics, including a blue-and-white plate purchased by Emperor Khai Dai. The living room is decorated with colonial-era lamps and traditional *gu* furniture.

Right There are two altars in this room. The one on the left is devoted to ancestors who came from China, while the one on the right, with the photographic portraits above, is reserved for more recent family members.

Opposite The area on the ground floor was once a dispensary for Thuoc Bac, Chinese medicine. It is now used as a reception room to welcome guests. It houses an impressive collection of blue-and-white ceramics. Traditional decorative wood and glass Chinese lanterns hang from the ceiling.

Above The layout of this house is typical of merchant houses in Hoi An. It follows a corridor plan, with house, small inner courtyard, then house, all in sequence. The houses are usually all timber-framed with either brick or wooden walls and tiled roofs.

Left This Hoi An house is later than most of the early merchant houses and reflects the growing French influence on architecture.

Right The narrow shady streets in Hoi An, bordered by picturesque dark wooden and tiled houses, are well organized and run in a grid pattern inwards from the river. The town's almost total absence of modern architecture and cars makes for a tranquil escape into a traditional way of life.

a chinese shophouse in hanoi

FOUND MAINLY IN HOI AN, and to a lesser degree in Hanoi, are a number of houses that illustrate the Chinese influence on Vietnamese building traditions. Around 1890 in Hanoi, the brick and stone dwellings of the city's merchants replaced the older structures of bamboo, wood, straw and other organic materials. Called "tube houses," they were mainly located in the middle of the 36 Streets and Corporations area, which has always been Hanoi's most lively shopping area. By the turn of the century, these houses, with their low, curved roofs, became synonymous with that particular area of Hanoi.

The term "tube house" arose because the house can measure up to 500 ft (150 m) in length, although their façades are only 6–12 ft (2–4 m) wide. This practice arose out of a taxation system that charged a levy on the street's occupancy and the density of the city. As a result, people opted to build two-story structures. Each contained a succession of identical multipurpose rooms, sometimes linked by a corridor, and usually a mezzanine in which to store merchandise or as rooms for not so important inhabitants. Internal courtyards, half protected against sun and rain by wood canopies, brought air and light into the houses. Sometimes these were converted into small gardens and were (indeed still are) used as ancillaries, as they usually lead into the kitchen.

A particularly noteworthy tube house, at 44 Hang Ga Street, is one of Hanoi's oldest houses of this kind that has been sensitively restored. As in many such houses, the second floor is the most prestigious part of the house. Here, one can view one of the most beautiful of Hanoi's ancestors' altars. In the Sino-Vietnamese sense of the word (*ban tho*), an ancestors'

altar is a set of liturgical objects used to worship one's ancestors: the wooden, rectangular lacquered tablets that carry their names, or their photograph; one big incense burner for the ancestors conceived as a whole, and as many smaller ones for each deceased family member not further back than three generations; flowers (in one or two vases); a pair of candlesticks; and a bowl of fresh water. These objects are set on a piece of furniture whose dimensions depend precisely on the date of birth of the head of the household. That piece of furniture is usually a shelf but, if the family is rich enough, it may sometimes, as in this house, look like a cupboard. It is then called a *tu tho*.

Opposite This "tube" house in Hanoi's old quarter has an internal courtyard which is used by the family as a garden and a place in which to relax and play chess.

Above Upstairs, an open corridor connects the front and back of the house, with wooden shuttered doors dividing the inside and outside areas.

Left The furniture in this room is in the traditional *gu* style. A cabinet stands on a heavy wooden bed which is used here as a table.

village houses

ALTHOUGH SOUTHEAST ASIAN civilizations have, or used to have, in common the use of pile foundations in vernacular architecture – primarily for air circulation and protection against natural or human threats – Vietnam's domestic architecture has evolved differently. Because Vietnam was under direct Chinese rule for more than a millennium, the Vietnamese adopted many Chinese traditions, including that of building houses on the ground. Much later, French colonial influence reinforced the adoption of these structures, stressing the so-called superiority of the European-style house over the "barbarian" house on stilts.

But Vietnam is a country where some fifty-four different ethnic minorities (20 percent of Vietnam's 75 million people) live, many making their homes and livelihoods in the spectacular mountains of the north and central highlands. Some of them, such as the Muong, the Tay and the Ede, have retained their traditional architectural patterns. Others have opted for ground-level homes, or, as in the delta areas, houses over water. Thus, all around Vietnam, to the delight of today's travelers, one can still see many different types of dwellings, all combining to show the richness of the country's varied ethnic groups and their architectural traditions.

There is, of course, a huge variety of village houses in Vietnam. They differ in shape, size, design and materials. Furthermore, since for many cultures a house is a place that is used as a continuum between practical and spiritual purposes as well as between private and public functions, almost each type of house represents a variation of how people conceive their life in this world. Vernacular homes in Vietnam basically perform two functions: they are where people live, but also where people worship their ancestors and spirits, the latter being the most important. These two functions determine a house's basic design, but other factors also influence its structure. Gender separation calls for different spaces for men and women, while social duties require a large, square courtyard in front of the house, where the inhabitants can organize huge meals if required. And, most importantly, a complex set of geomancy rules have to be strictly followed while building the house.

Pages 56–7 This Mong Phu house (above left), which was built 400 years ago, is 250 ft (75 m) long and 65 ft (20 m) wide, and is divided into three main living compartments. It is one of the best examples of architecture from this period. Apart from the tiled roof, the building is constructed entirely of wood. The altar dominates the central part of the house (right). To the left, which is traditionally the women's area, a small kitchen and eating area are now placed.

Above Blue shuttered windows and doors, cement tiles and coconut husk have all been used in the construction of this home in the Mekong delta area.

Right Fishermen's houses are often built along waterways, using coconut leaves and fibers as construction materials. As fortunes improve, zinc often replaces thatch on roofs. This is a typical scene along the Mekong delta.

Opposite This fishing village house on the island of Phu Quok is raised slightly above the ground on pillars to protect it from the sea at high tide. The construction of the building is in wood, each piece intricately carved and painted in the traditional Phu Quoc blue.

A particularly striking village house has been preserved in the village of Mong Phu, not very far from Hanoi. Built 400 years ago – as an inscription on the main beam testifies – the house of Nguyen Van Hung offers art historians and anthropologists an excellent opportunity to study the evolution of vernacular architecture in Vietnam. The house, about 250 ft (75 m) long and 65 ft (20 m) wide, is divided by four rows of six pillars, thus organizing the space into three traditional compartments. The six pillars support eight main beams, four lateral and four lengthwise, and twelve secondary longitudinal beams, all of which bear the tiled roof. Both ends are closed by a wall, which was added later, as up until the nineteenth century the use of bricks was restricted to members of the royal family and mandarins. The roof extends beyond the main body of the house, creating a veranda below, covered with stone slabs, which is as wide as the main façade.

Inside, the central compartment is devoted to an altar. This space is used as an area to welcome guests. The inhabitants and their guests normally sit on the mat that covers the trodden earth floor, or on the platform on the right, which may also serve as a bed. The right compartment, which in earlier times would have been reserved for the men, is now used as the sleeping room. The left compartment, being the women's space, houses the kitchen. Both compartments are separated from the main one by a beautiful and rare wooden panel and a temple-like door. The house does not have any windows, nor carvings nor superfluous details. Its austerity is nevertheless softened by Mr Hung's choice of two wading birds or *chim co* to guard the house, instead of the usual dogs. Such houses are, of course, very rare, but nonetheless an increased interest by both Vietnamese and foreigners in Vietnam has resulted in the preservation of vernacular forms.

A completely different regional variation can be found in the Mekong delta area where water, wood and plants mingle together to create a world where people live partly on the ground and partly on the water. Houses are simpler here than elsewhere, mainly because people spend more time on their boats than in their dwellings. Made predominantly from thatch, the buildings are used as living spaces, but also for storage and even as workshops where craftsmen build boats. The framework is simple: a beam supports an assembly of poles, most of the time made out of bamboo, on

which the roof is set. The decoration is often as simple as the design. True to Vietnamese tradition, the kitchen is always placed in a room next to the main house. As floods are a permanent danger, low dykes protect villages while houses stand on stilts. In contrast to other Southeast Asian peoples, the Vietnamese raised their houses only if they had no choice.

Another area that has a distinctive type of vernacular house is the island of Phu Quoc, 28 miles (45 km) southwest of Ha Tien and only 9 miles (15 km) from the Cambodian coast. Phu Quoc's 65,000 inhabitants are mostly fishermen, so villages are generally built next to the sea and under coconut trees which provide the necessary building materials – leaves for roofs and fibers for floors, walls, and interiors. The design of the houses, which are lightly elevated, is very basic, with one main room serving as the dining, sitting and sleeping room, with an adjacent kitchen. Surprisingly, the houses display quite elaborate decoration. As soon as they can afford it, the owners switch from fiber to wood. This allows them to design intricate façades, mostly painted in blue, since this color softens the light. The façades are shaped into three parts, the main entrance being flanked by secondary entrances or windows protected by wooden shutters.

Above left Each piece of this artfully decorated wooden façade has been hand-carved and painted blue and white, and is typical of architectural traditions on the island of Phu Quoc.

Far left and bottom right Inside, the decoration runs the gamut from calendars to curios such as wooden lobsters or strangely shaped stones, through the usual Buddhists images or posters depicting traditional tales, with the main emphasis being on pictures of the owners themselves. Each portrait is treated slightly differently. Here, the lady of the house is depicted in a setting illustrating domestic bliss, while her husband is portrayed as a successful businessman.

Above Even the metal security bars on the windows of this Phu Quoc home are designed to complement the delicate designs in the wood.

two hilltribe houses

MANY OF VIETNAM'S ethnic minorities, especially those living in the northern and central highlands, have taken pains to preserve their indigenous architecture. They have always tended to use lightweight building materials in their raised house construction compared with their countrymen in the lowlands who build low, sturdy wooden structures with heavy, flat-tiled roofs to withstand the annual typhoons. Moreover, most of these peoples traditionally never settled in a permanent place but moved over a relatively large territory due to the exhaustion of natural resources and the fertility of the soil after a few years of settlement. Their houses had to be transportable, easy to dismantle and to reassemble elsewhere, and were made entirely of vegetal materials.

The design of such houses, even today, depends mainly on the social organization of their inhabitants. Either the family chooses to live apart, in a stilt house, such as the Tay, or in collective housing, primarily a raised longhouse, such as the Ede. In the latter case, longhouses provide shelter for a certain number of families. The longer the house, the more wealthy and powerful the clan who dwells in it.

Regardless of size or shape, Vietnam's ethnic raised houses share certain similarities. Slatted floors allow for ventilation and for rubbish disposal (pigs often forage below the house), roofs are made of vegetable panels assembled together with rattan, fiber cords or bamboo strips, walls do not bear any load since the whole house structure lies on an assembly of posts and beams, and the interior is usually dark because the occupants spend most of their time outdoors.

Interior design also varies, depending on each group's auspicious orientation. Ede house entrances always face north and are only accessed by the men (the women have to use the southern gate). The correct position to sleep is to follow an east–west axis. The most sacred place is devoted to family heirlooms, unless these are kept in a separate place such as a clan house. The hearth is sometimes the center of the house, or it may be an inferior place only used by women.

The posts and beams of such houses may display carvings that have symbolic functions: stars, women's breasts, the moon, and various animals are quite common. However, not all houses are decorated. Decorative detail depends on the symbolic functions performed in and by the house, with these functions differing considerably from one culture to another.

The Tay stilt house and Ede longouse shown here were photographed at the Vietnam Museum of Ethnology on the outskirts of Hanoi, where an outdoor exhibition features the country's most popular indigenous architectural styles. The indoor museum displays collections of everyday objects (clothing, tools, utensils, weapons, musical instruments, etc.) from all fifty-four of Vietnam's ethnic minorities.

Page 62 The exterior of this Tay house shows how the windows and walls are constructed using woven panels held together with bamboo strips. The overhang in the roof is substantial to protect the house from rain. Removable bamboo poles allow the woven "shutters" to be closed.

Page 63 The stairway into the Ede house, with its carved motif of breasts, expresses women's power as a wife and mother and the importance of matriarchy in Ede society.

Below Inside this Tay house, the room is divided up using decorative woven panels to create walls. Bamboo is ubiquitous. Here, it is used to make stools for seating. The floor covering is split rattan.

Opposite above left The baskets hanging on the wall on the exterior of this Tay house on stilts are for holding sticky rice.

Opposite above center and right The beams of the Ede house are decorated with animals and fish. On the left is an elephant carving and on the right a turtle.

Below The interior of this Ede longhouse on stilts is laid out to accommodate an extended matriarchal family. The house is just over 138 ft (42 m) long. Benches made from huge old trees surround the interior fireplace. This area is used for receiving guests. Ceramic jars for drinking alcohol, with long bamboo straws, are set out in the middle of the room. The floors and roofs are in bamboo. The roof beams are skilfully carved with motifs of animals.

dinh community halls

Right and below Dinh Chu Quyen, also known as Dinh Chang (Trang), in the northern province of Ha Tay, is one of the most impressive buildings of its kind. The magnificent tiled roof, which curves upwards at the corners, is supported by a complex system of beams held up by vast wooden pillars, with a wooden floor covering the girders connecting the pillars. Probably built in the seventeenth century, it was restored in 1935.

Bottom left The heavy wooden doors of Dinh Tay Dang, also in Ha Tay province, are fitted onto wooden pegs which act as hinges. The area between the top of the roof and the door is heavily carved.

THE *DINH*, or traditional community hall, embodies the importance of village culture in Vietnam, playing an administrative, religious and cultural role. It was in the *dinh* that villagers discussed all village affairs, worshipped the village tutelary deities, performed cultural shows and organized ceremonies, rituals, meals, games and other village activities. Except for the administrative function, which now takes place elsewhere, the *dinh* continues to be at the center of the lives of Vietnamese communities. Vietnam's oldest extant *dinh* was built in 1576, but epigraphic and archaeological sources prove that *dinh* existed long before that time. The fact that their raised floors stand on stilts attests to the antiquity of such buildings, since Vietnam dispensed with houses on piles during the first centuries of our era.

Since the *dinh* is the most important building in the village, its site was always meticulously chosen following geomancy rules, as these determined its position, and there-

fore the wealth of the entire community. At either side and behind, it was supposed to have elevated terrain considered its "arms," and water in front in order to accumulate good fortune. Except for the roofs, *dinh* are made entirely of wood and display impressive carpentry techniques. Although there are only five different designs, assimilated to Chinese characters, *dinh* have many different styles. Local beliefs, influence from other religious buildings, distribution of space and other factors led to important evolutions, such as the presence of a rear sanctuary (or not), the number of compartments, the type and size of pillars, and so on.

Northern Vietnam *dinh*, such as the Dinh Trang and Mong Phu, tend to have a more austere look than central or southern Vietnamese *dinh*, which are usually longer. That does not mean that northern *dinh* are always older. Dinh Duong No in Hue is said to have been built in 1471, even though the current building was erected in 1808.

Basically, a *dinh* has one main hall with an altar at the back. It is divided into three compartments, the central one sometimes being larger, and two lean-tos. Rafters link either four (for the oldest *dinh*) or six rows of pillars. With time, a rear sanctuary was added to the structure to house the main altar. Some *dinh* have two sanctuaries, one in the front and one in the rear. A complex system of short and long beams stands on top of the pillars to support the roof, while girders

connect pillars and rows of pillars together. The floor boards cover these girders. Roofs are usually superb architectural structures due to a specialized structural arrangement that allows them to curve upwards. They are usually tiled, although one can still find a few *dinh* with thatched roofs. The roof's two main parts join at a top ridge, which is decorated with dragon heads made of baked clay. Non-decorated hips join the edges of the two main roofs.

Dinh community halls display impressive collections of carvings and sculptures. The architectural design that calls for tenons and bolts left many blocks of wood not only unused but also protuberant. Sculpture was hence used to transform these blocks into works of art. Some parts are more embellished than others, especially, but not only, the planks connecting upper and lower beams. These sculptures often display dragons, crawling or otherwise, or else details of a dragon's body. Fish, phoenix, deer, tigers, geckos, clouds, flowers, vegetables and scenes of life and festivals (hunting, wrestling, dancing and so on) are also popular subjects, testifying to the high level reached by Vietnamese artists from the sixteenth to the nineteenth centuries.

Since the *dinh* are places where deities (*thành hoàng*) are worshipped, they also house decorated altars and shrines, sometimes surrounded by wall paintings or sculptures of animals that are spiritually or symbolically associated with these deities, or which are powerful in themselves.

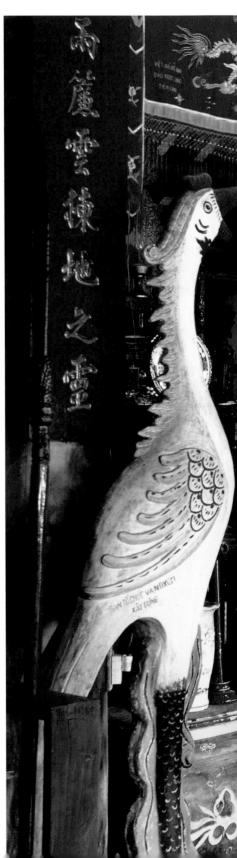

Above The floor in Dinh Chu Quyen has several levels, with both tiled and wooden surfaces. The central chamber is dedicated to the altar.

Opposite above left, and right The tiled roof of Dinh Phat Loc, located in the coastal province of Thai Binh in the Red River delta area, southeast of Hanoi, sags slightly in the center and curves upwards at the four corners. The altar inside the *dinh*, shown at right, is decorated with wooden sculptures and various ornaments that are symbolically or spiritually associated with the deities that are worshipped here.

Opposite above right Dinh Voliet, situated on a hillock near the border of Laos in Nghe An province, was built in 1858. The interior of the *dinh*, devoid of decoration on both pillars and beams, is thus relatively simple. However, Dinh Voliet is notable for its square courtyard surrounded by fifty-five ironwood pillars which support the community hall.

Above The roof of the Dinh Duong Nu in Hue is much simpler than the style of the roofs in northern Vietnam. The rectangular space in front of the building was probably once a lotus pond.

Left A pair of tall wooden sculptured and painted cranes flank the altar at the center of the *dinh*.

Right Tall carved and painted pillars hold up the roof on the veranda in front of the *dinh*.

Above Valerie reconstructed this traditional northern Vietnamese house as her office in the garden. All the timbers and tiles are original and were carefully reconstructed by a local construction team. The doors stand on a wooden base that runs along the façade and rotate around wooden pegs at the base and the top of the doorframe.

valerie gregori mckenzie vietnamese house

WHILE SOME VIETNAMESE opt to live in neo-French villas, some French prefer to settle in neo-Vietnamese houses. Such is the case of Valerie Gregori McKenzie, now a Ho Chi Minh resident, who decided some years ago to install her Hanoi office in a traditional Vietnamese house. She hired carpenters from a village in Ha Tay province to build all the house elements (wooden beams and posts and tiles for the roof), transport them to Hanoi and assemble them in her garden. Within a few months, the house was ready. The only concessions to urban requirements are the side and back walls that separate the house from neighboring buildings.

Valerie uses the house as a work space for her Hanoi studio and as a setting in which to display the wonderful linen, bags and other handcrafted objects she produces. Seen from the garden, the simplicity of the house creates a positive impression of sobriety, quality and solidity. Coming closer, one finds oneself on a veranda beautifully decorated with carvings and lanterns. On entering, one has to literally cross the threshold through the three traditional doors, since the doors stand on a wooden base that runs along the façade in order to protect the house's inhabitants from evil spirits and unwelcome crawling animals. Each door is made of three panels that rotate around a wooden post.

Inside, Valerie has maintained the three-compartment structure: in the central compartment there is a wooden bench and a few shelves displaying boxes, bowls and chopsticks. On the right side, surrounded by 1970s film and propaganda posters, is Valerie's desk, while on the left are displays of fabrics, clothes and household linen.

Below Valerie uses her traditional house to display her designs and to welcome her clients. Vietnamese domestic furniture and paintings, collected during visits to artisans' workshops in villages and traditional old houses, add interest and authenticity to the house. Valerie has been collecting Vietnamese artifacts since she moved to the country in the early 1990s.

suzanne lecht house

ART HISTORIAN AND COLLECTOR Suzanne Lecht needed a suitable setting in which to house her wonderful collection of contemporary paintings and older Vietnamese treasures. To this end, she acquired a traditional Vietnamese house in the suburbs of Hanoi and had a Black Thai minority (as this T'ai minority is known in Vietnam) house built on top of it. Her three-story dwelling is thus home to both ancient and contemporary art.

The contemporary art scene in Vietnam is very vibrant thanks to a rich tradition enhanced by a century-long dissemination of French art and techniques and the presence of many public and private art institutions, especially in Hanoi. Suzanne's collection is extensive and she takes great care in the placement of each and every painting. Doors open to reveal enigmatic portraits by young painters such as Pham Quang Vinh, Le Quoc Viet and Nguyen Quang Huy; scenes of pagoda festivals hang above a beautiful catholic altar from a deconsecrated church in Nam Dinh province; buffaloes and peasants watch over the dreams of those who rest on the traditional Vietnamese beds.

Wisely, Suzanne decided not to modify the ground-floor design. Here, the central compartment is devoted to an altar with the usual liturgical objects. But, true to her passions, she has placed a striking blue painting by Nguyen Quang Huy next to the altar, thus isolating it from the left compartment which is used to welcome guests. The right compartment also looks very traditional, with two custom-made benches and a table flanked by calligraphic couplets. Looks can be deceptive, though, as only one is genuine. Its (re)composed partner was commissioned by Suzanne from a Vietnamese man of letters.

Fusion asks for change. While the ground floor respects Vietnamese tradition and the first floor displays contemporary art, the top floor offers an entirely different atmosphere. Here, the Black Thai design surrounds everything from the roof structure to the furniture through the textiles and cushions that decorate the sitting room. Going up from the ground floor to the second floor, Suzanne can hence travel around Indochina.

Page 77 Suzanne reconstructed this traditional house on stilts from the northern village of Mai Chau on top of the second floor of her house. All the paintings seen in the room are by Pham Quang Vinh, one of the famous Gang of Five artists, including a self-portrait he did in 1996. Two nineteenth-century wooden statues, both female attendants to Buddha, stand to attention, one on the altar by the window, the other in the corner of the room. The textiles on the sofas are from Vietnamese ethnic minority craftsmen.

Left The carved trellised doorway leading to the outside terrace and pool area was designed by the owner when she built the house. Through the doorway, set against the wall, is a classical Burmese musical instrument shaped like a large bronze bell. The painting behind, also by Pham Quang Vinh, is entitled "The Musician."

Above The very fine nineteenth-century altar pieces used for ancestor worship which hang on this wall include two couplets in Chinese characters (representing classic Vietnamese writing, Nôm) flanking a gold screen which would formerly have hung behind the family altar. The style of the benches and table is typical of those found in traditional homes where they were used by the family to entertain guests.

Left The Buddha altar table in this room was designed by the artist Pham Quang Vinh. Standing next to it is a very special piece entitled "The Loving Buddha" by Nguyen Quang Huy, one of Suzanne's favorite artists. The oil painting shows a double-sided image of the seated Buddha with random text filling the canvas.

Right Above the day bed hangs a painting by Ha Tri Hieu, another member of the Gang of Five. To the left is a mixed-media piece by Nguyen Cam. A ceramic and oil gas lamp by the ceramic artist Nguyen Bao Toan hangs on the wooden pillar at the head of the bed. A collection of scroll paintings is also stored in this room.

Above Seen through the open doorway upstairs on the landing is an intriguing work by Le Quoc Viet. Titled "The Ego," it is painted as a scroll in Chinese ink on rice paper. What looks like a coat draped over the figure is, in fact, a series of hands.

Above Suzanne's bedroom on the top floor is her private haven. She has framed her bed with a nineteenth-century carved lacquer altar frame. An oil painting by Vinh entitled "Princess Mai Chau" hangs on the wall. Princess Mai Chau was murdered by her own father, King An Dong, one of the first kings of Vietnam, for betraying him to the Chinese.

khanh studio house

AN KHANH is a Vietnamese artist. Long before the area became fashionable, he purchased a plot of land in Gia Lam, the only suburb of Hanoi on the other side of the Red River, and built a house on it. Khanh wanted something different, so he bought a Muong house and had it erected on his piece of land. The Muong are amongst the oldest inhabitants of Vietnam. They used to form a single ethnic entity with the Kinh (the majority of Vietnam's population). By the sixth century, however, while Vietnam was under Chinese rule, the Muong decided to reject Chinese civilization and to maintain their traditional way of life.

Their houses are amongst the most beautiful in Vietnam's central and northern mountains. The design is simple: a central nave flanked by two narrower sides, a veranda running all around the house, and a ground floor used for whatever purpose one likes. As the interior is one long space, divided only by the roof's three sections, the inside is spacious. Like all other ethnic minorities' houses, it is made entirely of wood and is usually covered by a thatched roof.

Because Khanh is an artist with a large collection of installations and paintings to exhibit, his Muong house and the space surrounding it provide perfect display areas. The ground floor is a working and living place while the main room contains his collections. Installations made of stones, oil paintings and statues of praying worshippers, along with more traditional gongs, drums, jars and wooden tools, welcome visitors in an artful manner.

Opposite Khanh bought this beautiful Muong house and reconstructed it in Hanoi close to the Red River. The structure is quite large, with a ground and first floor and a veranda running all around on both levels. Typical of the Muong style, the interior is spacious, divided only by three sections in the roof. The house is made entirely of wood and has a thatched roof. A sole totem pole stands sentinel in front.

Above The entrance to the property is striking. Two large wooden figures flank the gateway, with tall steeples carved in wood overhead pointing up to the sky.

Above Upstairs, Khanh displays a collection of earthenware pots on the veranda that runs along the front of the house.

Right Sharing space with the family altar in the central chamber of the upstairs room are portraits of family and friends, large wooden statues of praying worshippers, traditional objects like jars and pots and antique wooden furniture.

Below Khanh uses part of the ground floor to display his large collection of installations and paintings.

loan de leo foster house

ONCE UPON A TIME, there was a small village in the outskirts of Hanoi called Nghi Tam. Situated near the West Lake, it was mainly populated by fishermen and horticulturists. Around 1918, one of them built a small lakeside house. This was restored by Loan de Leo Foster in 1995, when she decided to settle in Hanoi.

The work Loan did is hard to believe when one looks at the structure of the original one-story house. She started by rearranging its structure. While keeping the traditional Vietnamese division of three parallel rooms, she created three spaces that were separated yet united by ogival vaults supported by columns. The first space is a large dining room directly leading to the garden and then to the lake. The second is a cosy living room, while the third is split between the altar, which is the main part of any Vietnamese home, and an alcove housing a guest bedroom. Formally furnished with dark wood tables, chests of drawers, sideboards and lamps, these three spaces provide a warm and welcoming atmosphere, which is further accentuated by the yellow satin paint, reminiscent of Hanoi's traditional building color.

After a few years, however, Loan felt that something was missing. She then undertook, with the help of Vietnamese craftsmen, to add a true Vietnamese house on top of her existing one. If the ground floor evokes a mid-twentieth-century interior, one has only to look at the door that leads to the upper story to feel oneself in a time long vanished. Flanked by two painted statues of worshipping ladies in front of two vertical couplets (opposing calligraphy panels revered for their literary meaning and calligraphic value) and surmounted by a delicate painted glass lantern, the door itself is a masterpiece of carved and lacquered wood.

The world behind this door does not disappoint. A large room with tiles on the floor awaits the guest who simply does not know where to look. Should it be at the beautifully carved ceiling-height "moon gate" that separates the room from a discreet bedroom, itself leading to the most charming bathroom in Indochina? Or at the wooden panels that separate the room from a terrace where bonsai trees and ceramic ornaments are arranged? Or at the magnificent carved ceiling? It is difficult to know, because at every turn there are works of art, simple elegant furniture, paintings and statues – each as equally impressive as the next. Every corner reveals something new and splendid, a fitting testimony to how stylish Vietnam can be.

Left Not content with her initial restoration of the single-story house, Loan had an old Vietnamese home, which she brought from a village north of Hanoi, constructed on the flat roof of the original house. All the carved beams and doors are original except for the intricately carved "moon gate" which she added in order to separate the guest bedroom from the main room.

Right Apart from creating a second guest bedroom, Loan uses this space on the second floor as a place to welcome guests and to display some of her antiques. The golden seated lady, Ba Chua, is a particularly fine piece and sits in front of a Japanese scroll and two lacquered panels which are part of a set depicting the Four Seasons. The couplets here would have had very noble origins. The benches and low table are nineteenth-century colonial pieces.

Above The dining room, part of the new annex to the house, leads directly from the center of the house into the garden and onto West Lake. The two paintings seen on either side of the archway leading to the sitting room and ground-floor bedroom are by Bui Huy Hung. Both hang above two commodes that the owner bought in Taiwan. The china cabinet on the left-hand side is a French colonial piece found in Saigon. Loan bought all the Marelli fans in the house in 1989 and stored them with her aunt for a few years before she was able to use them.

Left Downstairs, in a small alcove off the sitting room, is the romantic guest bedroom. Loan commissioned the four-poster bed from an old Chinese design. The lamp in the foreground is by Valerie Gregori McKenzie, while the one nearest the bedroom is a Liberty bronze lamp found in Saigon. Like many houses in Vietnam, Loan has installed an altar for the Buddha which is also decorated with lacquered black and gold altar statues and Hue blue-and-white ceramics.

Right The wooden doors which form the entrance to the traditional Vietnamese house on the second floor were commissioned by Loan based on the design of the doors installed in her bedroom which came from a mandarin's house in Hue. The lamp is one of a pair of nineteenth-century Chinese-style hanging lights; the other is inside the new room. A large wooden frame, also an old Hue piece, forms a graceful archway over the entrance. Pairs of beautifully gilded couplets and painted statues of worshipping ladies flank the entrance.

Above left A secluded terraced garden was created upstairs when the old Vietnamese house was added. This is where the family have breakfast every morning. Bonsai trees and ceramic pots and animals contribute to the ambience of a traditional Vietnamese-style garden.

Left The dramatic guest bathroom features glazed air tiles for ventilation, antique mirrors, and specially commissioned washbasins with fish motifs inside based on the design of early Dong Son bronze containers, standing on reproduction red and gold lacquered imperial-style basin stands.

Above The new addition houses Loan's collection of Vietnamese ceramics, including blue-and-white shipwreck pieces. The bronze containers on either side of the moon gate are Han Chinese urns discovered buried in tombs in northern Vietnam. The day bed was bought in China.

Above The Chua Tay, at the foot of Sai Son Mountain in Ha tay province, 16 miles (25 km) south-west of Hanoi, is one of the oldest Buddhist temples in Vietnam. Originally built during the Ly Dynasty (1010–1224), most of the buildings still standing date from the early seventeenth century. The temple's tranquil location and bucolic atmosphere make it a delightful place to visit.

Far left and left Two beautiful horses stand at the door of the hall in the Chua Keo. The horses are used both as protective spirits and as creeds to the founding monk who went on horseback to the capital in 1061 to cure King Ly Thanh Tong of a serious disease. Each year the horses are used in the main ceremony of the temple's fall festival.

Above right The bell tower at Chua Keo is 38 ft (11.5 m) high and has three storys, each roofed with tiles that curve upwards at the corners. A large bell stands on each level.

buddhist temples

SPIRITUAL LIFE in Vietnam is a grand panoply of belief systems, including Confucianism, Christianity and a number of other beliefs created by mixing some patterns of these main religions with popular or animistic elements. Buddhism, however, is by far the most popular religion in Vietnam and the vast majority of Vietnamese are Buddhists.

Unlike its neighbors in Southeast Asia which follow what is known as Theravada Buddhism (Teaching of the Elders – the only surviving branch of the Hinayana (Lesser Vehicle) sect – Vietnamese Buddhism, as in Northeast Asia, comes under the Mahayana Buddhism (Greater Vehicle) branch. The main difference lies in the aim of the two sects. Theravada Buddhists only look after their own salvation through the cycle of reincarnation, the peak of which is nirvana, while followers of Mahayana Buddhism aim to attain enlightenment as a way of saving all other beings. Access to nirvana is possible only for monks under Hinayana Buddhism. The Mahayana doctrine, however, allows lay people to be enlightened thanks to the system of buddhas and boddhisattvas (those who have reached nirvana but devote themselves to save others).

Thus, Buddhist temples in Vietnam (*chua*) differ from those of their southern neighbours whose temples (*wat*) only house statues of the Buddha, Sidharta Guatama. In Vietnam, pagodas house a full pantheon of past, present, future and permanent buddhas as well as boddhisattvas. The statuary in Vietnam is therefore always rich, albeit often a little confusing.

The plan of a Vietnamese *chua* is rather simple: a courtyard that leads to the main temple extends from the entrance (which may or may not have a staircase), its portico and its three doors. The main temple is divided between the main ceremony hall where worshippers pray and an apse, both housing altars. Secondary halls house the altars of other deities. The basic plan can be modified by the presence of several courtyards separated by minor ceremony halls.

Buddhist doctrines emphasize the necessity for meditation, study and prayer. There are no Buddhist temples without a library of sacred texts, or at the very least a few bookshelves. They also all have empty spaces in front of their altars for prayer, and, most of the time, living quarters for those who have chosen the way, permanently or temporarily. Since some temples played the same role as abbeys did in Europe, they can sometimes resemble palace compounds.

Than Quang Temple, better known as Chua Keo, in Thai Binh province in the south of the Red River delta, not far from Hanoi, is one of Vietnam's most famous pagodas. A fisherman turned monk, returning from a year in Tibet, built it in 1061 as the Nghiem Quang Temple. King Ly Anh Tong gave it its

actual name in 1167. Severely damaged by floods in 1611, it was fully rebuilt in 1632. At that time, it comprised twenty-one buildings and controlled more than 22 sq miles (58 sq km) of land. Today, seventeen buildings, surrounded by a stone wall with a beautiful gate, still stand over a 2,200 sq ft (2022 sq m) plot.

The Chua Keo pagoda is built in such a way that the pilgrim has to proceed through a succession of gates, courtyards and secondary prayer halls before entering the main building where two seventeenth-century statues of famous boddhisattvas await. Like any other ancient Vietnamese building, the pagoda is entirely made of wood except for the tiles on the roof and the stone slabs on the floors. Wood, especially the ironwood used for temples, has many qualities: it is not hard to find, it burns slowly, it is solid, and it can easily be replaced without removing the whole structure. It is almost never painted, but is sometimes carved. Vietnamese pagodas have a severe, even ascetic ambience. This is lightly contrasted with golden characters in Chinese (the religion's writing), beautiful carvings and statuary.

As is often the case in Vietnam, Chua Keo is also a Taoist temple and honors the memory of its founder. Two beautiful recently restored wooden horses stand at the doorway of the second hall. Every temple is guarded by two spirits, one painted white to welcome believers, the other black (or sometimes red) to chase out evil spirits. However, statues of animals are frequently found in non-Buddhist temples, either because they symbolize a virtue or a quality, or because of their decorative value. In this case, the horses are used both as protective spirits and as creeds of the founding monk, who went on horseback to the capital in 1061 to cure King Ly Thanh Tong of a serious disease. Each year, the horses are used in main ceremony of the temple's fall festival.

taoist temples

TAOISM is a word that encompasses both the philosophy of the Tao (the Way) as well as religious, spiritual and sometimes magical practices. In Vietnam, Taoist temples called *den* are ubiquitous. Historical figures such as kings, generals or mandarins, deities belonging to the Taoist pantheon such as Ngoc Hoang (the Jade Emperor), Dien Mau (the Sacred Mothers) and countless spirits, are revered in them.

Some *den*, like Phu Tay Ho, situated on the shore of Hanoi's West Lake, follow the same basic architectural design as pagodas. The only difference is that their buildings are more highly decorated. The main entrance gate is always divided into three arcades topped by a painted pediment and a pavilion-like roof with upturned eaves. Inside the entrance gate, on the other side of a courtyard, stands the ceremony hall. Inside, the tablets of deities and other liturgical objects stand on top of the main altar, which is always carved and often lacquered in red and gold. Statues of the deities and other important spirits are placed on a second altar and framed by a carved wooden panel that features heaven.

Dynastic temples, such as central Hanoi's Ly Temple or the Dinh Temple in the old capital of Hoa Lu (968–1010), are also considered Taoist temples. In temples of this type, the main statue, which is always placed at the back of the temple, is an image of the king.

The Dinh Temple, which was first erected at the beginning of the second millennium and rebuilt in 1600, is Vietnam's oldest dynastic temple. Its plan follows the usual pattern: from the gate, an alley passes through a garden and a second gate to the temple fronted by an open portico. Rows of doors divide the temple into three areas. The first, which houses the altar of the king's parents, is also a meeting place for the temple servants. The second area contains the stele where the king's merits are described. Behind this, in the third area, is the king's statue and altar. Columns and pediments, beautifully painted and carved, depict dragons, spirits, the two guardians and scenes of everyday life of the time. Gongs, incense burners and ritual objects once used by kings and mandarins, called *bat buu* (the eight precious), and insignia of power, such as halberds, complete the temple decoration.

The Ly Temple, which was first built during the eleventh century, has been restored many times. It therefore looks more modern than most, but older touches, such as the side doors of the main hall carved with birds, the symbol of longevity, are evident. Inside, the living quarters resemble those of a pagoda, which is not surprising as the temple doubles up as a Buddhist place of worship. Buddhist texts and statues of boddhisatvas make this clear.

Hanoi's mixture of Taoism, colonial style and modernity sometimes results in an eclectic mix of architectural styles. To enter Nam Huong Temple, for instance, one has to go through a

neoclassical entrance hall that is copied after a colonial-era building. Beyond the hall is an 1888 statue of Le Loi, who established the Le dynasty in 1428. A protective screen separates it from the temple.

Hanoi's most famous temple is undoubtedly the Van Mieu or Temple of Literature. It is also called Quoc Tu Giam, the National Children's College. Built in 1070 by Ly Thanh Tong as a Confucian temple, it became Vietnam's first university five years later. It has been enlarged and restored many times. Its actual form follows the plan of the Qu Fu Confucius Temple in China. A two-story, late seventeenth-century stone portico leads to a succession of five courtyards symbolizing the five elements (metal, wood, water, fire and earth), and also a scholar's path to knowledge. One can go from one courtyard to another by three different gates, but in the Van Mieu all these gates have a symbolic meaning: Arts Constellation, Arts Crystallization, Success Gate and so on. The fourth courtyard or Sages Court, where chess is still played, is close to the Great Hall of Ceremonies where Confucius's altar is placed. Inscriptions, carvings and decoration all remain the worshipper of the Masters and his disciples' eternal virtue as well as the glory provided by Arts. Realistic or stylized dragons, once a royal, then a mandarin symbol, eventually became the insignia for the literary man whatever his social position.

Above This highly ornate sedan chair was traditionally used in religious ceremonies and processions to usher the gods. The chair would usually be carried by four people.

Left A gilded statue of the emperor dominates the hall behind the altar in the Dinh Temple, situated in the old capital of Hoa Lu. Vietnam's oldest dynastic temple, it was rebuilt in 1600.

Above The imposing main altar in the Dinh dynastic temple at Hoa Lu, set beneath an ornately carved archway and surrounded by heavily carved panels and exquisite gilt calligraphy, attest to the skill of artisans to create objects of beauty to venerate and dedicate to the Taoist pantheon.

Right top A large decorative parrot stands by the altar in the Dinh Temple, Hue.

Center right The Dinh Dynasty Temple in the old capital of Hoa Lu was first erected at the beginning of the second millennium, and rebuilt in 1600. It is Vietnam's oldest dynastic temple.

Below right The Temple of Literature has been extensively restored over the last decade. These beautifully decorated wooden doors lead into the main hall.

cao dai temple architecture

Above The windows in this Cao Dai temple, located in the Mekong Delta area, are brightly colored and ornate and run along the length of the walls of the building. The framed symbol in the center is different in each window.

Opposite A giant eye, the Cao Dai symbol representing the vision of all, beams down from the wall above the front entrance to the main temple, the Great Divine Temple. The Divine Eye is a recurring motif on walls and ceilings throughout the building. Painted panels depicting scenes of daily life adorn the doorway below the balcony. The building's eclectic style of color and design mirrors the strange mixture of religious ideals, and occur also at the main Cao Dai temple in Tay Ninh.

CAO DAI is a relatively recent addition to Vietnam's religious history. The sect was founded in 1926 by Ngo Van Chieu, a Vietnamese civil servant living in the Mekong delta, who purportedly had a passion for spiritualism and used ouija boards to communicate with spirits. In 1919 a spirit named Cao Dai appeared before him, telling him to combine the teachings of many religions into one to promote peace and to worship it under the form of an eye. Cao Dai, whose official denomination is Dai Dao Tam Ky Pho Do (the Great Way of the Third Era of Salvation), was officially recognized by the French authorities in the year of its creation, both because it became popular very quickly and the French thought it might be able to contain the country's chronic social unrest.

Cao Dai soon spread to southern and central Vietnam, but its capital city was, and still is, Tay Ninh. The sect has the equivalent of a Pope, who is called the Ho Phap, and a clergy attached to its temples. It is the best example of Vietnam syncretism known: Cao Dai recognizes and worships the deities of all other religions (Buddha, Jesus Christ, Taoist spirits) and major historical figures such as Victor Hugo, Joan of Arc and Sun Yat Sen. Its symbol, an eye, often at the center of a rectangle, comes directly from freemasonry. Today, Cao Dai has more than a million followers.

Externally, Cao Dai temples do not present any architectural originality since they look exactly like churches. Two bell towers flank the façade which is made up of a portico, a balcony, a pediment with the eye and a pagoda-like roof. A veranda usually surrounds the temple's two-story rectangular main body. The colonnade that circles it supports the building's weight, thanks to flying buttresses that reach the roof. The biggest temples may have a second tower at the back.

Caodaist interior architecture is more unusual. The nave is bare except for a single altar (a simple table) on which stands two candlesticks, a vase and an incense burner where five incense sticks remain burning along with sandalwood. The same liturgical objects are found on the main altar located in the apse, but they are joined by a specific Caodaist instrument called a beak through which Cao Dai himself speaks. At least two and sometimes eight columns surround the altar.

Caodaist design, distinguished by two main colors – gold and blue – is highly exuberant. Since the sect borrows from other beliefs, its temples present a good sample of Vietnam's most popular religious styles, especially Buddhism

大道三期普渡
ĐAI ĐAO TAM KY PHO ĐO

and Taoism. If the eye is always overlooking the altar, two guardians fully equipped with barb, helmet and breastplate guard the main door. Dragons, supernatural beings known to have carried Buddha, coil themselves up columns, while a set of seven tablets, directly issued from the Taoist tradition, stands on the altar. Before being able to get there, however, one has to go through a curtain-like panel sculpted with faces of the Caodaist main figures. The painting on the ceiling of the nave depicts the celestial residence of these spirits, while the West Heaven, the Sukhavati or "Pure Earth," where reigns Amitabha Buddha (infinite light), waits on the back of the entrance. Exterior decorations include paintings of peacocks, symbolizing the spirit, since they perch on the highest branches, dragons and the stylised character of longevity.

Opposite Like many Christian churches, this Cao Dai temple in the Mekong Delta area has a central nave and side aisles. The nave is empty apart from a simple table which serves as the altar. Disciples kneel on cushions on the floor. Fluffy clouds decorate the pillars and reach up to a painted sky. At the other end, the main altar is lit up with neon lights in yellow (representing Buddhism), blue (Taoism) and red (Christianity). Above the central arch sit the figures of Buddha, Lao Tzu, Confucius and Jesus Christ.

Below Another nave in the same Mekong Delta Cao Dai temple, is similarly decorated with an eclectic mix of objects, materials and colors. A pair of painted wooden storks and a matching pair of lantern stands flank the altar, which is set behind an elaborately carved and painted archway.

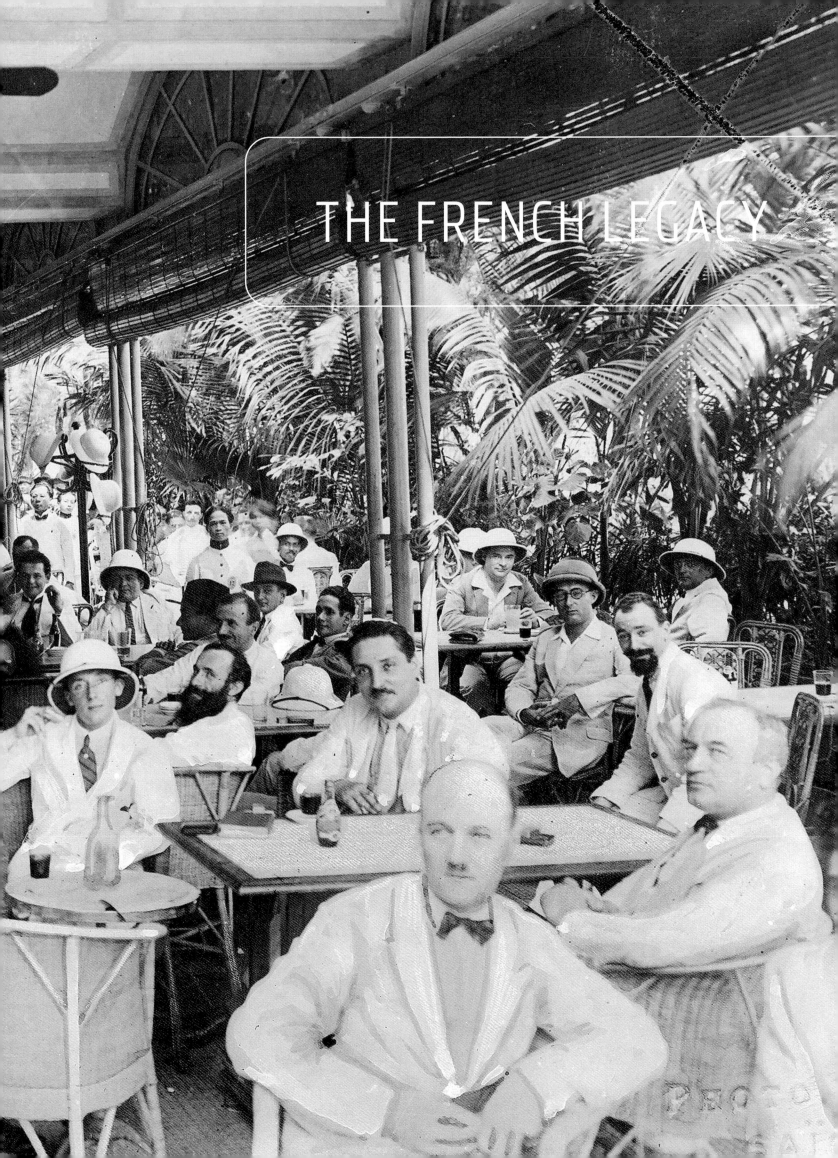

THE FRENCH LEGACY

Pages 102–3 A contemporary photograph depicting French colonial life in Vietnam. The men, dressed in typical linen suits and pith hats, enjoy an afternoon drink in a French bistro furnished with cast-iron tables and rattan furniture (both still popular today) to the sounds of a small orchestra.

Left Saigon's ornate city hall is one of the best preserved French colonial-era buildings. Built in 1901, it was formerly known as the Hotel de Ville and is similar in style to Paris's own town hall. It is a fine example of French colonial architect built to a neoclassical design. It is now the People's Committee of Ho Chi Minh City.

RESHAPING THE LANDSCAPE

Reshaping the landscape was almost certainly not uppermost in French minds on their arrival in Vietnam. But from that first landing, not far from Danang in 1862, through more than eighty years of colonial rule and endless transformation of the region, specifically of the cities, it was very much an outcome. Today, it seems as if the French have been there for centuries: French architecture, culture and influence is ubiquitous, from the north of the country to the south. Cities, railroads, canals and churches testify to France's will to transform Vietnam into a southeastern France – and to turn local towns into a little Paris. Although no part was left untouched, the French legacy is most noticeable in the cities, especially Hanoi (the capital city from 1901) and Saigon (now Ho Chi Minh City). This tradition continues today with people renovating old French villas, building colonial-style homes, and combining Western forms of both architecture and interior design with some local elements.

French colonial architecture was very much a city architecture, often duplicating without too much imagination French buildings from the *métropole*. Governors and mayors did their best to develop an "enlightened urbanism," with colonial homes lining avenues that led either to the cathedral or the city hall, if not from one to the other. All public buildings, including clinics, stations and hotels, were built to remind people that France was in charge. Architecture was a political tool, used as an illustration of the progress that the ruler thought it was bringing to the ruled peoples of Vietnam.

Neither imagination nor originality was needed in this type of architecture. Although neoclassic, neogothic, Art Nouveau and, later, Art Deco styles were all used, architects chose such styles not to demonstrate a sense of modernity but simply to follow the fashions of the day. Many of the tree-lined streets in the colony's towns, complete with arcades and coffee shops, replicated France's city avenues. Saigon's city hall looked very much like Paris's town hall. The Bank of Indochina building, now the Vietnam Foreign Trade bank, is reminiscent of the Trocadero palace. Hanoi's Opera House perfectly symbolizes both France's desire and ability to recreate a "little Paris" along the Red River. It was immediately coined "a little Garnier" because it more or less duplicated Paris's Opera House built by Charles Garnier. Its façade is massive, square and pillared – and the interior had an Art Nouveau staircase, a luxurious foyer, a huge 870-seat hall complete with loggias, and the latest technical facilities to match the best theaters in Paris (Italian scenery, sliding curtains, dressing rooms, and so on). Above all, the painted face of a Gallic warrior looked out from above the stage and faced the audience – as it still does today.

In this regard, there is not a great deal of difference between Indochina's various cities, especially Saigon and Hanoi. Since the manifesto mattered more than the buildings themselves, architects were not concerned with originality – the museums in Hanoi and Danang, housing the collections uncovered by French archaeologists, ethnographers and historians, being the main exception. The ability to duplicate a model was what they intended to acquire, which explains why we know so little about them. The names of such masters as Ernest Hébrard (probably the most famous among them as he received the "grand prix de Rome" and later directed the Indochina Architecture and Urbanism Central Department created in 1927), or Georges-Andre Trouvé are hence only known to a handful of specialists.

There are, nevertheless, some nuances. Civil guidelines regarding construction, the style of the building, and to a lesser extent local conditions imposed by the climate and the geography, exerted some influence on architects' choices. Saigon's Treasury, Hanoi's former Indochina Treasury (now the Ministry of Foreign Affairs) and the Bank of Indochina in Hanoi were all institutions devoted to the fiscal and financial procedures by which the French collected the capital they invested in Vietnam. But the buildings that house them do not look at all like each other. Saigon's Treasury was built at the end of the nineteenth century, and presents a striking similarity to the style that was used in the same era along the French Riviera. This was no mere coincidence as in both areas the climate was quite similar, even if the monsoon rains are unknown in France and if the heat is more intense than along the

Above left This well-preserved Hue villa, built in 1910, retains its original manicured garden. The iron pots, similar to those in the Imperial City, were used to burn offerings to the gods.

Below far left Hanoi is renowned for its grand colonial villas. Many of the larger houses have been renovated for official use while some of the smaller ones have been converted to restaurants or other businesses.

Below left Shaded parks and wide tree-lined avenues are a feature of all the main cities. In the evenings, the pavements are busy as people gather under the shade and meet their friends.

Above A colonial-era photograph of a rich French landowner receiving local dignataries who have come to present their credentials. The house is a typical blend of French colonial and domestic architecture with modern technology imposed by the gas lighting.

Left The Hanoi Opera house, one of the city's most striking landmarks, was built between 1901 and 1911. Harshly criticized at the time as a folly of grandeur, it nevertheless perfectly fitted French plans for both the urban reconstruction of the city and its cultural revival. It was extensively renovated in the late 1990s, and has been reincarnated as the artistic center of Hanoi, playing host to many Vietnamese and foreign artists.

Right The inside of the Opera House is not dissimilar to the Paris Opera House, although slightly smaller in size. There are ornate stairways and gilded mirrors, and boxes upholstered in red fabric, and a large stage to welcome performers.

Mediterranean coast. Before the advent of electricity, it made sense to use techniques that had shown their value and efficacy elsewhere. The other two buildings, which look almost contemporary in style, were built much later. But while, in 1931, Hébrard tried to give an indigenous look to what is now the Ministry of Foreign Affairs, a year before, Trouvé had successfully applied the precepts of the Art Deco style in order to underline the power of the most important, at least financially speaking, institution of Vietnam. A year later, the bank would be allowed to issue the piastre, the currency Vietnam used until the end of the French war in 1954.

The only buildings that deviated from this colonial form were the museums built by the French. These museums, whose aim was to cement the fusion of French science with Indochinese cultures, were carefully designed and built. What is now the Hanoi National Museum of History was first set up in 1908 as the Museum of Archaeology and Ethnography and was housed in the former General Governor Palace. (Later this was used as the Indochinese University.) In 1926, however, Ernest Hébrard was appointed by the EFEO to design a new museum building. It took seven years for Hébrard to build the Musée Louis Finot, so named after EFEO's first director. Hébrard, who was strongly opposed to the use of the gothic style used by his colleagues in Vietnam, tried to mix local influences with French architectural patterns. The result can be seen either as a pastiche of a Chinese building as understood by a Westerner or as a culturally sensible building that pays homage both to local architectural traditions and climate requirements. Whatever one's opinion, it perfectly exemplifies the "Indochinese style" that became the Hébrard trademark. The same can be said about the Cham Museum in Danang. Built in 1916 by Henri Parmentier in order to shelter the EFEO's collection of cham statues, it was extended in the 1930s and inaugurated in 1936 by the Emperor Bao Dai. Since its location was first designed to be a garden, the museum was built as an open-air space with the idea that visitors should feel more that they were in a park than in a classic museum. This kind of setting, where the arts of Vietnam were showcased with immediate access, was not usual. Generally architects preferred to stick to classical formulae. But in this case, probably because Henri Parmentier was also the main collector and researcher of the art displayed in the museum, an attempt was made to match the method of display with the "soul" carried by the objects.

French influence was also very much in evidence in the villas built along the broad avenues flanking the centers of Hanoi and Saigon. Although at first glance many colonial villas look quite similar, there are certain variations. On closer inspection, it becomes clear that the original owners took pains to build and decorate them according to their own individual tastes – and sometimes elements of their professional lives. Former Navy officers inserted porthole-like windows or shaped the main balcony or the house as a shortened prow, neogothic adepts flanked their houses with a pinnacle or turret, while former residents or aficionados of Deauville or Biarritz built villas in the style of those in Normandy or the Basque regions.

As these houses belonged to and were built not only for the French bourgeoisie, but also for the local bourgeoisie, elements of indigenous architecture are also evident. House-building followed complex rules, especially in Vietnam where geomancy was highly respected, so many details that look purely ornamental are, in fact, the physical manifestations of *phuong thuy* principles. Carved panels between the gate and the entrance of houses, corner or side entrances, the awkward positioning of trees in front of the house and other devices were all designed to protect houses and their inhabitants from evil spirits. Maybe the application of such *phuong thuy* rules has actually protected these houses, because a great many remain – even after half a century of revolution, wars (including fierce street battles) and neglect. More likely, however, it was the builders' technical expertise in taking the climate and environment into consideration that has contributed to their survival.

Right The Government Guest House, opposite the Sofitel Metropole Hanoi on Ngo Quyen Street, was built by the French architectural adjutant in Hanoi, Auguste-Henri Vildieu, in 1895 as the Palace of the Resident Superieur, and is one of Hanoi's best preserved architectural heritages.

Left Beautifully restored, like many of the important buildings in Hanoi, it has large green painted wooden shutters. The real delight is in the entrance with its decorative wrought iron and glass porchway.

symbols of french power

NOWADAYS THE GOVERNMENT GUEST HOUSE, mainly used as a place where the Vietnamese government receives official guests, symbolizes the political changes that deeply transformed Vietnam during the twentieth century. To understand the building's history, however, one has to go through the complex system the French devised in order to rule over Indochina.

Formerly Indochina was divided into five parts. Only one part, Cochinchina, now Vietnam Southern Region, was a colony. The other four, Cambodia, Laos, Tonkin and Annam, were "protectorates"; the kings of Cambodia and Laos and the Vietnamese emperor were still the legitimate rulers. In order to advise them about the best way to rule, the French flanked them with Residents Superieur, men who reported directly to the Governor General of Indochina. In Tonkin, now Vietnam Northern Region, the Resident Superieur advised the Viceroy who represented the emperor, whose capital was then in Hue. Since these men represented France's highest authority in the Protectorate, their residences naturally had to symbolize this power. At the time it was built, the Palace of the Resident Superieur was the biggest stone building in Tonkin and had the most magnificent staircase in Vietnam. Three years later, however, it was superceded in size and grandeur by the Palace of the Governor General.

Auguste-Henri Vildieu erected the Palace of the Governor General on Ngo Quyen Street in 1895. It mixed Napoleon III and Art Nouveau styles in a neoclassical synthesis that would later become very fashionable. At the time, however, its main purpose was to showcase French technical superiority over their Vietnamese subjects. The building was a political statement that was supposed to carry an explicit threat: see what we are able to build and beware our power!

For more than forty years, the Palace of the Resident Superieur symbolized French rule over Vietnam's oldest city. In addition, it was the place that housed French power over northern Vietnam. It was therefore hardly surprising that the August 1945 Revolution made the building its main target. The storming of the building on August 19 showed to the thousands of Vietnamese who had rallied in the city for several days that the revolution would be successful and that Vietnam would eventually get its independence. For the same reason, Ho Chi Minh, who became Vietnam's first president in 1946, chose it as his office, instead of the more pompous former Palace of the General Governor, which he did not like. Much later, he decided to move into a small wooden house built in the park that surrounds it, but the former Palace of the Resident Superieur always kept its political charge.

Right The striking mustard-colored Presidential Palace in Hanoi was built between 1900 and 1906, also by Auguste Henri Vildieu, as the living and working headquarters for the French Governor General of Indochina. Like most French colonial architecture, the palace is decidedly European in style and stands behind high wrought-iron gates flanked by two sentry boxes. When Vietnam achieved independence in 1954, Ho Chi Minh refused to live in such a grand structure, although he still received state guests there, and he eventually built a traditional Vietnamese house surrounded by carp ponds on the grounds of the palace. Today, the palace, which is not open to the public, is used by the government for formal and important meetings.

sofitel metropole hanoi

Left The Hotel Metropole, now the Sofitel Metropole Hanoi, was the place to stay in Hanoi from the moment it opened its doors in 1901. Famous guests have included Graham Greene, Somerset Maugham, Charlie Chaplin, Noel Coward and, much later, Jane Fonda. The hotel has been carefully refurbished over the years and retains many of its original features. The old wing still has its polished floors and grand staircase, with a patterned carpet custom-made to the original design. A large chandelier hangs down from the ceiling and lights up the reception hall.

Above A painting of the hotel in the 1930s showing its recently reopened outdoor terrace hangs in the lobby. All the furniture in the hotel has been made to reflect the original pieces of the period.

Top right Built by two private French investors, the hotel quickly became the rendezvous for colonial society. The façade, with its green shuttered windows and sweeping entrance, has hardly changed since the hotel was built. Today, guests can slip back into history riding in the back of the hotel's old Citroen or in a renovated cyclo.

SOFITEL METROPOLE HANOI – the former Metropole – was, and still is, one of those legendary hotels whose name represents more than the place itself. Built by two entrepreneurial French businessmen in 1901, opposite the Palace of the Resident Superieur in the heart of Hanoi and within walking distance of the famous Hanoi Opera House, it immediately became the rendezvous for colonial society as well as "the place to stay" for visiting heads of state, ambassadors, civil servants, army officers, writers, entrepreneurs and the first tourists keen to see "the pearl of the French Empire." It was refurbished in the 1960s and again in the 1990s – the latter in order to receive the influx of French tourists attracted to the country – and the hotel – following the release of evocative films like *The Scent of the Green Papaya* and *Indochine*.

They were right to go there. Every room, including the Graham Greene suite where the author partly wrote *The Quiet American*, has kept its original wooden floor, and the Beaulieu, the very French restaurant of the hotel, provides the same atmosphere it had in the mid-1930s, mainly thanks to its Art Deco style. The façade, built in 1901, has not changed, nor the splendid staircase that some intrepid guests prefer to use instead of the more sensible, but not so romantic lifts that were a later concession to modernity.

Even if you do not stay at the Sofitel Metropole, a visit to the hotel is worthwhile. Sipping a coffee (what else?) in the café, or else a papaya juice in the garden, with a little imagination (provided you ignore the new wing) you can feel the atmosphere that made Vietnam the dream it is now. It somehow beggars belief that under the name Thong Nhat (reunification), the hotel was for decades a place where rats were as comfortable, if not more so, than guests.

The Sofitel Metropole Hanoi is, in fact, probably the only place where travelers can find the perfect mix of French style and Vietnamese smile. No other hotel in Hanoi provides such an experience, since none is as venerable.

temple club

THE TEMPLE CLUB was opened in 2000 and has quickly established itself as one of downtown Ho Chi Minh City's most stylish bars and restaurants, in Ton Thap Tiep Street, an area that is a rapidly developing with new shops, restaurants and apartments.

What makes the Temple Club so different from others is that it has attempted to create something akin to the city's heritage. In 1880, the Chetty Community, East Indian traders and money-lenders who began to settle in Saigon towards the end of the nine-teenth century – built themselves a Hindu place of worship, the Mariamman Temple. Directly opposite, they built a large three-story building as a dormitory and refectory to welcome pilgrims.

The owners of the Temple Club, Luc Lejeune, Stella So and Lee Baker, were determined to secure the second floor of this build-ing as soon as they saw it, although it took some years. The trio had a very clear idea of what they wanted to do with it, which was their own interpretation of the Indochine theme with all its nostal-gia for playful Art Deco functionality and seductive decoration. It had to be a comfortable and stylish location to meet friends and clients. All the furniture and fixtures were sourced by the owners, pieces were commissioned, and local markets were scoured. The building was gutted, the red bricks were left exposed, and new floors were added. All the rooms were personally arranged by the owners until they were satisfied that the décor looked authentic but not old.

The well-disguised entrance is reached along a lantern-filled passageway which leads to an elegant doorway opening up to the entrance hall, which typifies the mood of the whole club – a felicitous mix of contemporary and Indochine style that reflects a romantic yearning for those glamorous days of the Art Deco period. The hall leads to the splendid long bar, carefully created using mainly reclaimed wood from old houses. Small private dining rooms at the front lead to the main dining area and into the Club room, which is laid out with all the intimacy of a private home.

This philosophy has contributed well to the sense of comfort and style of the place. Every item is a vintage design collected by the owners, and many of these original pieces have been repro-duced for clients. This is where guests feel genuinely at home, sitting back in oversized sofas and deep leather Art Deco-style armchairs, all designed to individual specifications.

Left The Art Deco-styled sofas and chairs in the Temple Club are based on 1930s designs and were created to Temple Design's specifications. The custom-made light-ing, an important aspect of the club's interior, was inspired by old lamps found in antique markets. The paneled lacquer painting on the wall possibly came from India via the East India Company. Scattered throughout the art-filled rooms is an eclectic mix of artifacts, including books and small bronze incense burners used as ash trays, all salvaged from various places.

Left The staircase in the reception hall was moved to create a large reception area. The Art Deco chandelier, imported from Hong Kong sometime during the 1950s, was sourced in Hanoi. A Khmer head sits on top of an old Chinese cupboard. Behind it, on the wall, hangs a Chinese shophouse mirror advertising its business.

Right The small private room at the front of the restaurant was originally an open-sided terrace looking down onto the noisy street. The traditional handmade encaustic red and green tiles on the floor were reclaimed from an old French villa. The dining furniture was all made by Temple Designs. Most of the pieces in the club are reproductions of antique pieces that Luc has collected over the years.

Left This unsigned painting, dated 1942, is believed to have originated in the Ecole des Beaux Arts d'Indochine. It depicts a fortune-telling scene with a girl praying in front of a pagoda. The Temple Club is full of furniture which has been reproduced by Temple Designs, including this stunning deep red Chesterfield sofa, to produce a look of studied comfort and elegance.

Left In order to break the monotony of the exposed bricks, large wooden screens which are back lit and hung with silk, hang on the wall. Ceramic wall lights, similar to Dutch colonial lamps, provide additional lighting. All the tables and chairs in the restaurant were custom-made by Temple Design.

Above Above the piano hang two Chinese advertising posters bought in Shanghai. The unusual lamp on the piano was designed by Temple Design. Through the doorway on the left is a view of the private room, which is separated from the main dining room by reclaimed wood-framed glass doors.

Right The lacquer painting, rescued from a dustbin, hangs over a beautifully crafted wooden cigar cabinet, a contemporary piece made by the French designer Jacques Blanchard, who lives in Ho Chi Minh City. The 1930s wind-up gramophone is by Pathe Marconi, the French company that eventually became EMI.

Left The entrance to many of the houses of the French colonial period was often up a small staircase, with the main reception rooms being on a raised ground floor. This was to allow air to circulate in the basement area and to avoid humidity.

Right The house was renovated in the mid-1990s by the first European Union reprentative in Viet-nam at that time, to replicate as closely as possible the original features of a 1920s home. The original panneled smoking room, now a cosy living room, opens up into a larger reception area which leads through to the dining room. All the ceiling lights were reproduced from one original light that was still in the house. They are made of copper and glass. The furniture was all designed in imitation of the Art Deco style.

eu ambassador's residence

WHAT IS NOW THE RESIDENCE of the European Commission Delegate in Vietnam was formerly the residence of the Deputy Director of the Bank of Indochina (the Director's house is now the Italian Embassy). Hence it was not the largest house in Hanoi, but nevertheless it is a good example of an upper middle-class villa from the 1920s. Typically, its facade, which is a bit brighter than it used to be seventy years ago, presents the basic elements of this type of architecture. Features include a huge balcony on the second floor, a mix of rectangular and arched doors and windows, sometimes flanked by porthole-like openings, and brick canopies above these windows, positioned so as to prevent rainwater from soaking into the house.

As was customary, again as protection against water and humidity, the house is not entered at ground level, but via a small staircase. Almost all such villas were built with an entresol, the main reception rooms being on a raised ground floor; below this was a space where air was able to circulate, thus ensuring an even temperature and a minimal degree of humidity inside. From every room in this residence, large windows afford views over the garden, inviting the beauty and coolness of the tropical vegetation to add space and light inside. In fact, the subtle relationship between the exterior and the interior is the house's main charm.

The interior is also typical of this kind of villa. The second floor was, and still is, kept for private use housing bedrooms, bathrooms and so on. The first floor, however, is organized as a reception area, with a dining room, living room, a smaller room that used to be the smoking-room (life in French Indochina followed strict rules of etiquette) and the entrance hall, from where one could reach these rooms. A recent renovation added the kitchen to the main part of the house, but in earlier days, as is still the case in rural Indochinese houses, the kitchen was housed in a smaller structure some distance from the house proper.

Other notable features are the high ceilings and ceiling fans, both useful antidotes to heat and humidity, and the attractive fireplace, a bonus during North Vietnam's chilly winters. Two beautiful old lanterns grace the entrance hallway and the former smoking-room, but elsewhere ceiling lights are modern, although in keeping with the style and atmosphere of the house. The display of antique ceramic jars, a few Chinese calligraphy pieces and custom-made classical-style wooden tables and chairs help to create or re-create an ambience that the former residents would probably have appreciated.

Above The house has a huge covered terraced balcony on the second floor which looks over the lush tropical garden below. Downstairs, there are port-like doors leading into the house and small porthole windows, a style popular in the 1920s.

Right This house, originally built for the Deputy Director of the Bank of Indochina, was designed to host large parties in style. Only the reception and sleeping quarters occupied the main building, while the kitchen and staff quarters were located in an adjoining annexe. Today, the kitchen is in the basement and the reception rooms upstairs have been returned to their original splendor.

Opposite The large dining room is ideal for formal entertaining. The table is a reproduction of a classic French colonial piece, and is surrounded by Vietnamese styled chairs. The carpet reproduces the same "key" design found on traditional Vietnamese furniture. Each of the reception rooms is cooled by its original Marelli ceiling fan.

psyche kennet house

PSYCHE KENNET'S THREE-STORY HOUSE is a good example of the merging of colonial and contemporary styles. Situated in one of Hanoi's most charming boroughs to the north of its oldest area, the main part of the house is separated from the kitchen by a small courtyard, thus paying respect to Vietnamese tradition. Well stocked with ornamental plants and shrubs, it is also the source of light for the interior.

The living and dining rooms are situated near the courtyard, and have the feeling of an interior garden. Psyche has managed to retain their original character, which comes mainly from the beautiful floor tiles, the fireplace and the generous height of the ceiling, and has decorated them with just the right amount of furniture and nothing more. The heavy dark wood furniture is complemented by two wonderful standard lamps, whose feet used to be temple pedestals for the various emblems that usually flank the altar. Their orange lampshades give a soft diffused light to the dining room, and match the color of the room's main painting.

The upper stories are accessed via the original wooden staircase, a handsome feature in itself. Here, the ambience is altogether more contemporary, with modern furniture and colors setting the tone. Of particular note is the attic bedroom, a space characterized by a modern bed, rattan bedside tables and wicker trunks – and a wonderful blue palette that is accented in the carpet, the bedspread and the paint color on one wall. Other bedrooms are also quite contemporary, although one features a colonial-style niche in front of the room's main window. Here, two low dark wood armchairs and a small square table perfectly introduce the urban landscape – a tableau marrying the old with the new.

Left The upper stories are accessed by the original wooden staircase, an impressive structure which smakes its way up the stairwell between the high-ceilinged rooms.

Right The standard lamps, once temple pedestals, are an example of the fusion of old and new which characterizes much of contemporary Vietnamese design. The elegant lacquer painting by Bui Huy Hung, one of Vietnam's leading contemporary lacquer painters, also mixes the past and the present to create a modern Vietnamese style. The tiles, which are modern, are influenced by the types of designs found in parts of southern France. The table and chairs are typical of the Indochina style, merging colonial and contemporary designs.

Above The attic bedroom is contemporary in design, with a blue color theme running throughout, as seen in the handmade carpet and bedspread as well as the art. A collection of traditional embroidered bags hangs in the corner of the room.

Left The living room, adjacent to the inside courtyard, retains much of its original character through its original floor tiles, high ceilings and painted brick fireplace, a welcome feature during Hanoi's harsh winters. The room is sparsely decorated with two plantation chairs, a standing Morelli fan, and an old clock.

Right Upstairs, two low dark wood armchairs and a table, reproductions of 1930s Art Deco furniture, sit in front of tall shuttered windows, looking out onto a view of Hanoi's rooftops and courtyards.

Left The magnificent staircase in the center of the house, built of terrazzo and concrete in a combination of Art Nouveau and Art Deco styles, forms a delightful contrast to the checkered French cement floor tiles below. An altar holding a statue of Buddha and a bowl for burning incense are perfectly positioned in the curve at the bottom of the stairs.

Right These brass handles are on an old Art Deco cabinet which was left behind by the owners of the house when Valerie and her family moved in. The house was built in 1953 by a Vietnamese architect, Pham Dinh Bieu, the father of the present landlord, in an area of Hanoi which was a reclaimed swamp.

valerie gregori mckenzie house

IF ONE IS LOOKING for a mid-twentieth century Hanoi villa complete with colors, furniture, paintings and tiles, one need go no further than Valerie Gregori McKenzie's house in Hanoi, which perfectly represents a genuine "colonial" atmosphere that is full of fantasy and taste but allows for comfortable contemporary living. Right from the entrance, the visitor is struck by the harmony created by the pastel colored walls. Indeed, the whole house is painted in a combination of light blues, greens, oranges and yellows that give individuality to each of the rooms yet link the house into a coherent whole. The same can be said of the original French cement floor tiles, which present a variety of colors that match those on the walls. In contrast, the door frames, window frames and shutters are painted a neutral green or gray.

The house was designed and built by a famous Vietnamese architect, Pham Dinh Bieu, in 1953 in a mixture of the Art Deco and Art Nouveau styles that were quite fashionable during the last decades of French rule in Vietnam. The large round, distinctly Art Nouveau windows throughout the house are reminiscent of a boat's portholes. What would be the boat's prow is a magnificent staircase that is partly Art Nouveau, partly Art Deco, linking the two stories of the house. Its upper part is well lit by a "trellis" comprising three columns of small square openings that also provide air circulation. The main part of the house is divided into various sections and corners, rather than rooms as such, which are multi-functional. Hence, the kitchen also serves as a dining and living room, the main living room also acts as a library, one of the bedrooms is a conveniently laid-out office, and so on.

This flexibility is achieved mainly by the careful positioning of sets of furniture. Paintings, posters, lamps, ceramic pots, books on arts and design, and other carefully chosen items from the colonial era, ranging from clocks to old car models, set the tone. The furniture, with its painted panels, original brass work and dark wood, offsets the pale walls and decorative flooring. The combination also allows for the creation of a patchwork of ambient corners. The best example is probably the set created around a circular window, whose form is matched by two clocks, three small square paintings and a few objects placed upon a cabinet whose shape complements the porthole-like window perfectly.

Right Valerie found this old painting in the house, which is painted in the style of Modigliani, probably by a student from the former L'Ecole d'Indochine. The wooden candle sticks and lacquered pot painted with water lillies sit on top of a Chinese-style cabinet in the main hallway upstairs.

Below Valerie had the bookshelves made locally. The ceramic fruit sitting on top of the left-hand one are traditional altar decorations used during Tet festivities. On top of the other cabinet is a collection of Chinese ceramics. The painting, by an unknown artist, depicts Hanoi's main railway station in 1961. Like a lot of propaganda art from this period, it is a depiction of industrial strength in northern Vietnam.

Above The upstairs sitting room is furnished with 1930s Art Deco ironwood furniture left behind by the owner. The cement tiles are typical of the style of the 1950s, and are much simpler and more graphic in style than earlier periods. The painting on the right is by Nguyen Thi Trung, one of the most famous artists of L'Ecole d'Indochine, who is known for his portraits of young Vietnamese women in *ao dai*, the traditional dress.

Right The porthole style of the round window in the dining room is repeated throughout the house. On the right is a painting by the northern painter Phan Ke An, dated 1976. The photographs are from the American Vietnamese photographer An My Le. The large clock on top of the dresser is a 1950s promotional clock used for advertising which Valerie found in an old department store in Hai Phong city in the early 1990s.

135

Left The tall wooden doors and large shuttered windows in Valerie's bedroom provide good ventilation. The gilded chest of drawers is by the designer and furniture maker Richard Forwood. Above hangs another propaganda painting from Valerie's collection, this one from the 1980s depicting a tram running through the center of Hanoi.

Right The staircase on the second floor leads up to a large terrace. The Chinese lamp, made from oil paper and hand-painted with Chinese characters, is from Hoi An. To maximize the amount of ventilation flowing through the house, the architect created a trellised effect in the wall for the air to circulate freely. Unlike windows, they do not let in hot sunlight.

Left A series of wood-framed glass-paned doors leads the eye through the house and out into the garden. The car is an old toy found in a public garden which was being used as a prop by a local photographer. The yellow and orange colored tiles on the floor were designed by Valerie to replace the original damaged flooring.

catherine denoual
& doan dai tu house

SOUTHERN VIETNAM'S climate may be wet, it may be hot, but it is never cold. Architecture, therefore, has to provide protection against the sun while allowing for the greatest possible air circulation. If air conditioning is not an option, high ceilings and wide openings work well. Catherine Denoual and her husband Doan Dai Tu applied these traditional methods when they designed their house a few years ago on a large plot of land not far from Ho Chi Minh City.

They built their palatial residence with the help of Luc Vernet, an architect living in the city whose main passion is designing boats. Luc designed the complicated roof structure with its open ceilings and wooden rafters. The house is composed of a central structure with wings radiating from both ends, each terminating in a square pavilion sandwiching a swimming pool; this combines the traditional role played by a pond with cool air rising from it and flowing into the house, but it also provides a vista of cool. Most of the central structure comprises a large hall that leads to a veranda through three large openings. The 12 ft (4 m) high hall is topped by an exposed roof which facilitates ventilation. The outside veranda, which can be used throughout the year, doubles as a dining room, the kitchen being located at its left end. Both wings house various bedrooms and offices. While a guestroom is located in the right-hand pavilion, the other pavilion ends with a duplicate of the veranda, a wooden sitting room where one can enjoy the coolness and beauty of southern Vietnam's evenings.

A small thatched-roof pavilion originally on the site was retained and has been refurbished. Separated from the main house by a lotus pound and a wooden bridge, it provides local helpers with a quiet environment in which to relax.

Left The front entrance to the house leads directly to a large 12 ft (4 m) high central hallway, which forms the heart of the house, and straight through to a veranda, large garden and swimming pool at the back of the house. The house is designed for open living, its lofty, exposed wooden ceilings and rafters and the large door opening facilitating ventilation and allowing light to flood the space. The piano was found in a music shop in Saigon, as well as most of the furniture which Catherine reupholstered with fabric she bought in Paris. The wall lamps were designed by Catherine's design studio.

Above The large veranda outside the main entrance hall in the middle of the house looks out onto the garden and pool. It is used by the family as a dining room. The cement tiles were based on an old French tile design.

Left A small wooden bridge crosses over the lotus pond and leads to a charming thatched-roof pavilion which is now the staff residence.

Above The outdoor sitting room pavilion sits adjacent to the master bedroom in the nearest wing of the house and is used by the family to entertain guests in the evening. It also provides useful shade in the daytime next to the pool area, making it a quiet corner in which to relax.

Right The master bedroom in the far wing of the house leads off the garden and pool area and is cool and functional. Glass-paneled sliding doors lead into an equally calm bathroom area. The four-poster bed was found in an antique shop in Saigon.

hien house

A VIETNAMESE SAYING describes the three conditions for happiness: eating Chinese food in a French house with one's Japanese wife. Mrs Hien, who lives in Hanoi, does not exactly follow this advice, preferring to live a Vietnamese life in a French villa. But her lifestyle is nonetheless a synthesis of Eastern and Western styles – as is her house.

The house, which was built in 2000, looks French. The design would have pleased the most demanding nineteenth-century Parisian. From top to bottom, the house offers everything that is requested by the canons of Western interior architecture: the ground floor is reserved for social life, while bedrooms are on the first and second floors. The windows, balconies, curtains and chandeliers would also have perfectly fitted the salon of Marcel Proust's aristocratic friends.

But the same Parisian would have found the house's atmosphere rather "exotic." Since Mrs Hien owns an antique gallery, she has tastefully picked all the items displayed in her house. Ceiling fans, a beautiful wooden staircase and calligraphy hanging from the walls of the ground floor exemplify another culture. But the ambience owes its Vietnamese characteristics mainly to the harmony between the wooden pieces of furniture and the contemporary paintings.

Three parts of the house are especially interesting: Mrs Hien's bedroom displays a dark tonality, from the bedspread to the paintings to a superb wardrobe. The upper part of the wardrobe is made of wooden strips that provide air circulation, a smart way to fight Hanoi's high humidity, but also allows the traditional *ao dai* tunic that Hien sometimes wears to become part of the décor. On the first floor landing, a set of late nineteenth-century armchairs and table perfectly matches a mirror that was, not so long ago, used by the actresses of one of Hanoi most popular theaters. And the loft offers those courageous enough to climb there a very simple but warm Vietnamese setting. With a large coffee table and four cushions, Hien has managed to create a type of boudoir where courtesans in the past could have felt perfectly at ease.

Above left A beautiful wooden staircase, its walls enhanced by picturesque black-and-white scenes of Hanoi's old quarter, curls up to the upper stories. Tropical house plants sit in the well of the staircase, offsetting the severity of the staircase and square-framed photos.

Above The ground floor is reserved for the sitting room area. Wooden calligraphic panels hang on the wall flanking a lacquered altar-like buffet piece in the middle of the room. On top are displayed two fine ceramic vases. The contemporary sofa and armchair in darker tones match the traditional Chinese-style coffee table, with its a black-veined marble central panel.

Below Mrs Hien has chosen tasteful contemporary pieces for her dining room. The beautifully lacquered chairs around the wrought-iron dining table match the large lacquered landscape that dominates the room. The chandelier adds a French touch.

Right A collection of delicately carved antique picture frames are hung at the bottom of the landing of the staircase. Through the doorway can be seen a cabinet displaying Mrs Hien's treasured ceramics.

Far right At the top of the landing, visitors are welcomed by a small charming seating area. A lacquered mirror sits above a wooden occasional table inlaid with mother-of-pearl. Two large carved wooden chairs complete the arrangement.

Below right Mrs Hien's bedroom combines Eastern and Western styles. The carved bedstead reflects the continuing French influence in design executed by Vietnamese artists and designers in the post-colonial period.

MODERN TIMES

Pages 146–7 A large family portrait of the Khanh family (page 182) hangs alongside a portrait of Michele d'Albert, both painted by Quasar Khanh. The aluminum and glass console and dining table and chairs are Quasar's creations.

Right The furniture in Spa Tropic was custom-made by the designer Le Cuong. The pieces are a modern interpretation of plantation furniture mixed with early 1920s Art Deco. The celadon green-colored tiles in this renovated French villa were made in a factory outside Hanoi.

ECHOES OF THE PAST

Vietnamese style today is a collusion of the many architectural and cultural influences that the country has absorbed over the last several hundred years. Borrowing simultaneously from the styles of the past and using traditional Vietnamese techniques and creativity and combining these with modern designs and structures, today's eclectic "Vietnam style" represents both something old and something new.

For ten years following the end of the American War in 1975, most people still faced difficult times and few had the time or the inclination to pay attention to creativity, let alone architecture or interior design. But after fifteen years of *doi moi* – the country's open-door policy – a period that among other things brought about a policy of cultural renewal, people began to pay closer attention to their lives and their surroundings.

Traditional urban house styles began to undergo modification to make them more contemporary in style but also more practical. New features were added, such as glass ceilings and paneled walls, wooden parquet flooring and new concrete tiles, in an effort to create a more comfortable environment. Certain traditional Vietnamese conventions and observances, such as the bonsai garden or an altar table, still played an important part.

Modern apartment buildings are now becoming a feature of the Vietnamese architectural landscape, particularly in Hanoi and Ho Chi Minh City. Apartment living is a fairly new concept in Vietnam. Although some buildings were put up in the 1960s and 1970s, these were relatively few and were mostly located in what was then Saigon. Today's apartments are usually in purpose-built structures, such as that of Catherine Denoual and Doan Dai Tu (page 172). The couple were able to work with the architect Herald Duplessy to create a very large space in the center of the city on top of a newly constructed department store.

Other residents, such as Michele d'Albert and Quasar Khanh, embraced the colonial style and cleverly converted an existing villa into a refreshing modern living space (page 182). It is encouraging to see many of these villas being rescued from destruction although there are many that are still being demolished. The history of these villas covers more than a century, from the mid-nineteenth to twenty-first centuries, and is an extremely important part of Vietnam's architectural heritage. However, restoration is time-consuming and expensive and usually involves the complete renovation of the villa to preserve the original architectural style, appearance and structure. This includes removing and replacing all of the utility systems in the building, including all electrical wiring and plumbing. At the same time, many modern service functions, such as a kitchen, need to be installed as originally they were not designed to be in the main part of the house.

Some colonial villas are being restored using reclaimed structural elements such as window frames, shutters and door hinges, and fixtures such as ceiling fans and lighting which have been repaired to working order. Ho Chi Minh City resident Lawson Johnston has been involved with many of these restoration projects and has spent much time collecting bits and pieces from demolished houses in his efforts to rehabilitate other old villas.

New cement tiles have been designed to fit existing flooring patterns and colors and terracotta roof tiles are made in beehive kilns in the Mekong delta. Traditional limewash paints are also used to mimic the original hues.

Resort development, a totally new concept in Vietnam, is also beginning to make its mark. The site of the Evason Hideaway on the picturesque Ninh Van Bay is a good example (page 166). Taking full advantage of its dramatic setting, the resort has developed its own architectural style which strongly reflects the traditions of Vietnam. This is immediately evident on arrival in the reception area and also in the dining pavilion, which are both classic examples of Vietnamese structures transported across the water and assembled onsite. The inspiration behind these traditional structures was only made possible with the assistance of local craftsmen whose knowledge of centuries-old building techniques is still being practiced by a few.

Traditionally, Vietnamese homes have never contained much furniture, just the basic necessities of a bed, altar and table for the family to eat at and for entertaining visitors. This changed radically during the 1930s and today furniture plays an important part in the modern Vietnamese home where appearance is often more important than comfort.

A lot of the furniture popular today is Chinese in style, such as the traditional heavy *gu* furniture which is also being reproduced by local craftsmen. But pieces from the late colonial period, now defined as "Indochine style," are also popular. At the beginning of the 1990s, collectors began scouring the markets and antique shops for furniture and other antiquities, including art. Designers began to create objects that were influenced by the past but totally modern in their construction. Luc Lejeune was a pioneer in his approach to collecting and design (page 158). Some of the earliest pieces he retrieved were being discarded by their owners, some in good condition, others in serious need of restoration. His collection soon included furniture and paintings as well as statues, buddha images, silver and glassware, mirrors and other decorative items. Some pieces, particularly furniture and lamps, he adapted or reproduced for his clients, and through this he developed his retro-Indochine vintage style which has influenced many later designers.

More recently, these traditional-inspired designs have been complemented by modern pieces made from materials like cast aluminum, recycled plastics and resins. The well-known designer Quasar Khanh, for example, has created a collection of sand-blasted aluminum furniture based on designs he first started working on in the 1960s. Despite the "globalization" of such designs, however, both sophisticated Vietnamese and expatriates continue to realize the potential of local cultural sources, workmanship and design elements in homes increasingly viewed as tranquil refuges from the outside world.

valerie gregori mckenzie & rene tayeb house

VALERIE GREGORI MCKENZIE moved to Hanoi in 1992 with her then husband John McKenzie. It was the slow pace of life back then that seduced her. Vietnam was just beginning to open up to the world, and both Ho Chi Minh City and Hanoi hummed with the sound of rickshaws, bicycles and Honda 50 scooters. The shackles of Communism were rattling and business was booming. It was a country on the move, a country of opportunities.

Inspired by the exceptional standard of the handiwork she found on her travels around the countryside, Valerie set up her own fashion business, Asia Song Design, in 1996 in a shop in Hanoi's pretty Nha Tho Street. A second shop followed in Saigon, which eventually persuaded her to move to the city permanently in 2001, although she still maintains her Hanoi studio in an old Vietnamese house (see page 72).

She now shares her house, Fort de l'Eau, on the banks of the Saigon River with her boyfriend and business partner, Rene Tayeb, and her children, Tara and Aubrey. Fort de L'Eau was built during the mid-1960s for a rich Vietnamese family as a weekend retreat away from the bustle of Saigon. By the time Valerie found it, the current owner had rented most of the garden out as a café, known as the Love Café, where young Vietnamese lovers would come on their motorbikes to conduct their affairs in private.

The house, not far from creeping suburbia hidden behind a high wall, is one of the most original and peaceful homes in Ho Chi Minh City. The colors of the interior are rich and vibrant and the style and architecture all reflect Valerie's upbringing in a timber-framed plantation-style house in the Caribbean.

An outdoor kitchen and dining area, set out on a large wooden terrace, afford the widest possible view of the Saigon River. Tables are cluttered with ceramic pots collected from all over Vietnam. Books and maps spill out of tall bookshelves commissioned by Valerie, and paintings by Vietnamese artists, many of them friends, hang on walls or are stacked up in corners.

The bathroom, screened by banks of tropical plants, is separated from the main house. There is no modern plumbing as such, only a large Japanese-style wooden tub and shower. Nonetheless, this is a place of tranquil creature comforts.

Much of the garden had to be completely redone, particularly along the riverfront where the ground had eroded to such an extent that the ancient swimming pool had to be filled in to prevent the daily tide from flooding it. The area has been raised and is now covered with a large wooden terrace overhanging the river.

Left In the outside kitchen facing the Saigon River, modern appliances share space with a traditional clay oven and open shelves hold a miscellany of kitchenware and decorative items. Blinds separate the dining area filled with a terrazzo table and benches used in the former café.

Below The bathroom, a separate structure in the garden containing a Japanese-style bath and shower tucked behind a stone slab wall and sink unit, reflects Valerie's love of local materials and artifacts and her flair at combining these with modern amenities.

Above Valerie's children chose the décor for their bedrooms. Her daughter Tara elected for a blue and yellow color scheme and decorated her bed with her mother's bedlinen designs. The Chinese cartoon characters on the wall were commissioned by Valerie and painted by a local artist.

Right The colonial-period bronze head was found in an antique store in Hanoi. The painting, by an unknown artist, is very traditional in style and depicts one of the gates into the Hue Citadel.

Above Aubrey's room is painted a more masculine yellow. A self-portrait hangs on the wall. The walls and floor are all made of broad old timber planks. All the windows in the house look out to the garden and beyond to the Saigon River.

Right The embroidered velvet curtains and cushions on this sofa were designed and produced by Valerie, and are typical of her style. The painting and lamp are also her designs. The ceramic jug was a gift from a French potter.

ford foundation house

A FEW YEARS AGO, a French architect built the Ford Foundation director's house on the shore of Hanoi's West Lake. Borrowing simultaneously from traditional Vietnamese architecture and modern design, he created something entirely new. Local design is respected, although slightly modified, in regard to the partition and placement of rooms. The central hall, which performs the role played by a Vietnamese house's central compartment, is flanked by living quarters hidden by white walls. On the south side of the house, which faces the lake, a traditional veranda allows for an outside sitting room from where one can see a beautiful garden and the lake.

Vietnamese traditional house patterns are also used in the roof structure. Four longitudinal sections of seven beams, each one supporting a part of the roof, duplicate classic architectural frames. But the architect has entirely modified this pattern by adding a large ceiling at the center of the house. Pyramidal in shape, it is composed of concrete and glass and invites the daylight in; furthermore, it overlooks a Zen-looking garden whose white sand contributes to disseminating the light. Unlike a Vietnamese house, therefore, the building's *raison d'être* is shaped and symbolized by a marriage of wood and light. Wooden parquet flooring, windows and French door frames, posts, pieces of furniture, and even the façade's pediment, are all illuminated by the light that flows into the house.

Such a setting is ideal for the furniture that exemplifies Vietnamese modern design with function. For instance, a black lacquer screen is used to hide a modern office, whose equipment would clash with the house's style. And on the other side of the main hall, another screen is composed of a light bamboo frame draped with Thai textiles – an artfully created vernacular combination.

Below left The house was constructed combining traditional materials and modern construction techniques to create a contemporary functional living space. The back of the house faces the West Lake. An ornamental garden leads down to the water's edge. The paving in the garden is made from red brick.

Below A glass skylight in the traditionally constructed roof adds light and a feeling of space. It also draws attention to the rock sculpture, a feature of old Vietnamese homes. The tiled floor and wooden pillars are from an old house in Ha Tay province.

luc lejeune & vu dinh hung apartment

THE HOME OF LUC LEJEUNE and Vu Dinh Hung stands stoically on the corner of one of Ho Chi Minh City's busiest trading intersections. Built at the beginning of the 1920s by a wealthy local businessmen, like many of the houses of that period it served as a large family residence as well as a business premise, with the all-important shop front on the ground floor.

As soon as they saw the building, Luc and Hung decided to make the second-floor apartment their home. Although it was cramped and gloomy, with extensive and skillful refurbishment of the interior, Luc has transformed the four-room apartment into two bedrooms plus a large living and dining area in order to accommodate his precious collection of antiques and to suit his lifestyle. The colonial profile of the house dictated much of its decorative style. The proportions of the main room turned out to be extremely generous, dominated as it is by tall doors and wooden shuttered windows. The tiled floors throughout the apartment are all original.

Luc started collecting antiques the day he moved to Vietnam in the early 1990s. He was a pioneer in Vietnam in his approach to collecting, with some of his earliest pieces being retrieved from the French Consulate building after they were discarded during renovation. Quickly his passion turned into a business as he discovered more and more pieces, many in need of serious restoration.

Traditionally, Vietnamese homes did not contain a lot of furniture and this did not really change until the 1930s when, through French influence, it became fashionable. Much of what Luc has collected came from this late colonial period and is now defined as "Indochine Style," a mixture of Vietnamese and French or, as he likes to describe it, a "bastardized version of the Louis XV (instead of a French classical motif, local artisans used symbols such as that of double happiness) and the late Art Deco style." By the 1940s, furniture factories like the well known Than Le Company were producing high-quality pieces for the home market and also for export.

Most of the furniture collected by Luc is made from very good quality timber, mainly tropical hardwoods. His furniture is complemented by an eclectic mix of accessories and *objets d'art* reflecting both his and Hung's travels around the region and an obsession with collecting. Luc's exceptional taste has found favor with style enthusiasts in many parts of the world, and has followed him into other ventures, including the stylish Temple Club (page 118).

Above This sideboard, which came out of the dining room of the French Consulate when it underwent refurbishment, along with other pieces of furniture in the apartment, is framed by a collection of family photographs and a painting of an unknown northern Vietnamese girl.

Above right An Art Deco-style dining table sits on a fine hand-woven rug, probably produced by Hang Khanh, a prewar factory in Hai Phuong in the north. It came from one of the official residences of the last emperor of Vietnam, Bao Dai. A nineteenth-century ancestor portrait picked up in China adds color above a collection of wooden Buddha images.

Right Above this chest hangs a portrait of a bourgeoisie Vietnamese woman from the 1960s, thought to be Tran Le Xuan, the infamous sister-in-law of the first president of South Vietnam. Two busts from the Bien Hoa School of Fine Arts stand on pedestals either side of the chest.

Far right The old divan bed dominating this room is made from rosewood, which would suggest that it was produced in the southern part of the country where this type of wood is more prevalent. The bedside tables are Sino-Vietnamese. A lovely Chinese ancestor painting hangs above the bed. The carpet in front was picked up in Armenia.

richard forwood house

THIS CHARMING HOUSE, which sits camouflaged behind water palms and coconut trees along the banks of the Saigon River, is the realization of a lifelong dream for the English furniture maker Richard Forwood. When Richard first moved to Ho Chi Minh City in the early 1990s, he lived in a gardener's hut on the roof of a run-down hotel while he looked for the perfect plot of land on which to build the house of his dreams.

It took nearly ten years before Richard was able to find a suitable piece and embark on his vision. Once he had found it, it took another two years before he was able to commence work. First, 2,000 trucks of earth had to be brought in, not only to fill up the swampy land but also to shore up the riverbank which was fast being eroded by strong currents from the Saigon River. Then came the design. Not surprisingly, having lived in the country for so long, he could not fail but be impressed by traditional architectural techniques and craftsmanship. The initial inspiration came from the Temple of Literature in Hanoi, one of Vietnam's oldest buildings, and one of the first university buildings to be built in Southeast Asia. From there, he added elements from various European and Asian designs that he admired – "a colonnade here, a courtyard there, a Chinese fret or an eighteenth-century gilded paneled room."

The building team comprised a long-suffering Nguyen Anh as contractor, Le Duy Long as technical expert, Nguyen Vaa Xi, an experienced engineer and craftsman who had spent much of his career renovating the Imperial Palace in Hue, and Do Thanh Nam, the project manager and draftsman, who lived on site. Together, piece by piece, the project took shape.

Built entirely of local Vietnamese hardwoods, in particular *muong*, which was adopted by the French and planted throughout their coffee plantations to protect their crops, the two-story wooden frame was finally erected at 4 o'clock one morning on the advice of a Buddhist monk who presided over a simple ceremony and conducted prayers.

The spacious house is constructed to encourage airflows and cool living spaces. A large veranda runs around the exterior of the building, with each main room opening on to it to catch the river breeze. Stepping through the front door into an open courtyard, with its sunken pool and frangipani tree at the entrance, guests are led into a central hallway with lofty paneled walls and teak floors constructed from garden furniture offcuts produced at the owner's factory.

A mix of eighteenth-century style English furniture, gilded mirrors and local handicrafts are scattered throughout the interior. Almost all the furniture was designed and manufactured by Richard. He is also a keen gardener, an enthusiasm inherited from his parents and his rural Irish upbringing. Tropical growth is constant, and within a relatively short time an exuberant jungle of exotic plants and trees had sprawled around a lawn leading down to the river edge, an unusual feature in Vietnam.

Left Louvered shuttered doors around the ground floor of the house open directly onto the broad veranda. The fretwork on the glass panels is taken from a traditional Vietnamese woodwork design.

Below The spacious veranda is the heart of the house, where most activities from eating breakfast to evening drinks take place. The large dining table, made from an old Vietnamese bed, can seat eight and is surrounded by teak chairs produced at Richard's factory. Curtains can be drawn for privacy or to moderate sunshine and heat. The manicured lawn is a highly unusual garden feature in Vietnam.

Left Cool river breezes flow through the hallway in the heart of the house, which is open on both sides. Here, Richard displays his collection of fine furniture. A large Vietnamese aquarelle landscape hangs on the wall above a handsome chest of drawers.

Below The front entrance to the house opens directly to a cloister-style garden courtyard graced by water fountains and a thirty-year-old frangipani. This leads into the main hallway in the center of the house. The black slate used on the floor is from Danang. Two bedrooms lead directly off this central area as well as the kitchen.

evason hideaway

THE EVASON HIDEAWAY spreads itself quietly across Ninh Van Bay, a private cove accessible only by boat in an undeveloped area on the Vietnamese coast. The site was chosen by the manager who had been hosting languid picnic parties on the beach for a number of years. It is easy to see why. Arriving there is like discovering your own private island, with white sandy beaches and clear blue waters set against a mountainous backdrop of tropical trees and vegetation. A large wooden jetty welcomes guests as well as the daily supply boats, which include the local fishermen.

Most new construction in Vietnam is done without regard for local architecture or indeed the environment. Here, the owners have stuck to their belief in simplicity and sustainable development by being sympathetic to both, without compromising comfort. The design is very much contemporary but the inspiration behind the resort reflects traditional Vietnamese elements and local craftsmen's knowledge of centuries-old building techniques and appropriate materials. As with most Southeast Asian vernacular building traditions, structures rely heavily on the use of timbers, natural woven materials and bamboo. Wood is everywhere, from the vast pillars and beams in the traditional *dinh* (community) style house where guests are first taken on arrival, to the wooden floors throughout the villas and the deep wooden bathtubs. Old timbers were sourced from around the country, including Vietnamese *muong* and teak from old houses which were dismantled and then reassembled. Local sustainable woods were used in the various pavilions housing the library, bar, dining room and spa as well as the rustic furniture, which was designed and built on site.

Almost all of the essential elements of tropical living are here. Some of these elements are dictated by climate, such as the high roofs and deep eaves to cope with the heavy monsoon rains. Others elements are dictated by lifestyle, with large indoor and outdoor bathrooms in each of the villas, privately situated in their own gardens among coconut trees and a profusion of tropical plants. The most spectacular of these villas are built on the rocks at either end of the bay and are only accessible by boat.

Water, another key element, forms an integral part of the landscape, appearing in imaginative plunge pools set into the rocks and hillside, and from a stream that meanders down the mountain and into the spa.

Page 166 In front of the restaurant, a wooden boat is moored inside a small sandy bay to take guests back to their bungalows. Each room is constructed on rocks alongside the shore on a point at the end of the bay. Private dinners are held on the beach with a grand view of the bay.

Above left The reception area, built entirely of wood with a woven coconut palm ceiling, is designed to represent a traditional Vietnamese village community hall. The floor is made of tinted concrete, imitating the colors of Nha Trang beaches. The sofas and benches, all made on site, are covered with handwoven textiles in natural dyes.

Below left The bathrooms in each bungalow are half inside and half out, with their own individual gardens planted with locally sourced plants. The bath tubs, which were made in Vietnam, are an imitation of traditional Japanese bath fixtures. All the sinks and taps are made of copper and built into a wooden table.

Below Each two-story thatched villa has its own pool and is set in its own garden between the ocean and the tropical mountain forest – an all-in villa concept which emphasizes romance and privacy. A large daybed provides a place to take tea and gaze out through the tropical garden to the sea beyond.

Above and right The Rock Villa provides guests with various bathing choices, both inside and out. In the center of the bathroom (right) stands a large wooden tub from where bathers can enjoy a view of Ninh Van Bay. A door leads out to a wooden sundeck where a terrazzo plunge pool, built seamlessly into the rocks (above), allows bathers more stunning views of the bay and distant hills.

Above right In the simple beach villa bedrooms, mosquito nets are hung from a bamboo frame, while louvered doors slide open to private pools. The unbleached cotton hand-embroided curtains by Valerie Gregori McKenzie provide additional shade and privacy.

Far right The bathroom used by guests next to the swimming pool has a truly ecological feel, with everything built out of natural products nestled among the rocks and trees. The floor has been constructed using colored concrete and sand and is dotted with wooden stepping stones.

catherine denoual & doan dai tu apartment

WHEN THE GAYA DESIGN TEAM decided to set up their flagship store in one of Ho Chi Minh City's up-and-coming regenerated streets, Ton That Tiep, two of the partners, Catherine Denoual and Doan Dai Tu, decided to convert the space on the top floor of the building into one of the city's first modern classic apartments. The space is a continuation of the shop below.

Designed in conjunction with architect Herald Duplessy, Catherine and Dai Tu wanted something which was in total contrast to their home in the Vietnamese countryside. The apartment is fresh and inspiring, creating its own magic despite a spartan shell and a no-frills interior. Color, texture, form and line all work together in perfect harmony. Great care has been taken to ensure that everything in the apartment is in perfect alignment; there is a reason for everything that has been chosen and placed.

This is a place of light, which streams in through oversized windows with views out onto one of Saigon's early twentieth-century Indian mosques. Ultramodern lighting has been added, creating layers of mood which change throughout the day. The white concrete floors and walls are accentuated by light and glass, and are used judiciously to create a peaceful living space, typifying a commitment to purist form and function over ornamentation.

The walls and floors are also used cleverly to break up the simplicity of the space: a single aluminum wave-shaped line laid into the concrete floor carries one's eye from one area of the apartment to another; while a large wooden painted panel hangs on the wall of the main living area, creating a graphic neutral colored surface reflecting the curves in the floor. Another contrasting streak is a long white leather sofa dominating this area. Jolts of brighter color add spice to the otherwise neutral interior, with funky 1970s inspired furniture, such as the white plastic molded chair and orange lacquered coffee table. The floor's wave-like pattern leads visitors upstairs where the linear and white themes are continued along the corridor leading to both Catherine and Dai Tu's bedroom and their children's. The only items interrupting this flow are musical instruments and the children's workstations, but even they somehow do not interrupt the rhythm.

The bathrooms have not escaped the owners' minimalist approach. The children's bathroom is designed to be fun but easy to maintain, while the owners' bathroom is large and well equipped, although, like the rest of their home, everything in it has a purpose.

Page 172 All the furniture in this out-there sitting room was designed by Catherine and manufactured in Vietnam. Lighting plays an important part in the aesthetics of the room, from the natural light flowing through the large windows to the light fixtures which are her own designs.

Left There is no clutter in the living room. Each item has been carefully selected and positioned, such as this simple vase with lotus flowers and the rose-colored acrylic lamp on the lacquer-topped side table.

Above Two resin Buddha statues, internally lit, are set into small alcoves in the wall. Whilst they are not very large in size, they produce a calming glow subtly visible out of the corner of one's eye as one moves around the room.

Above right A Victorian chandelier hangs over the marble-topped dining table laid with colorful contemporary lacquer and glassware by the designer Michele d'Albert. In the corner is a 1970s-inspired molded chair, an icon from that period of design. The large windows which run across the front of the building ensure that the dining room is always bathed in light during the day. At night, the room enjoys the reflections of the city's lights.

Right Catherine's own range of bed linen in the master bedroom forms layers of texture and color, creating a haven of sensuality. A screen designed by Lawson Johnston diffuses the light in the room.

Below Most of the furniture in Tran Manh Dat's house is made out of locally produced ironwood in the Ming style. There are various statues around the room, some representing the Buddha in different seating styles. Others are painted temple statues. He also has an impressive collection of Vietnamese ceramics, both blue-and-white and plain earthenware.

tran manh dat house

TRAN MANH DAT is a man worth knowing. Not only is he one of Hanoi's best photographers and the owner of a wonderful antique shop (see pages 180–1), he is also the proud owner of a house that is inhabited by more spirits than humans. These take the form of an exquisite set of rare and ancient statues, each respectfully displayed. There are also some wonderful pieces of furniture and a collection of paintings that portray the association between ancient and contemporary in a manner rarely seen in Indochina.

The décor is all the more noticeable because Dat's house – one of those three-story modern cubicles that are so common in Hanoi today – is not architecturally exceptional. However, he has maximized its possibilities. Entry to the house is through a large French window; facing north, it provides just the right light for a small altar-like table where a Buddha image is flanked by two late nineteenth-century figures in prayer. The Buddha is in the Abhaya-Varada mudra, symbolizing the absence of fear, indicated by the raised right hand and the act of giving with the left. On each end of the table stand two stylized bronze cranes, the crane being one of the Taoist symbols for longevity. Behind the table hang paintings by Nguyen Tu Nghiem, one of the four masters of twentieth-century Vietnamese painting. Nghiem, who is still alive, is famous for his semiabstract animal paintings, and here his works tastefully complement the statuary. Other Buddha images are displayed on stands and a bench to the right of the room, amongst ceramics and lamps and behind a rare eighteenth-century square wood table. To the left of the altar-like table is a cabinet, itself a masterpiece of craftsmanship, containing a superb collection of eleventh- to twelfth-century vases.

The second floor of the house is replete with other treasures, including a rare spirit chair. Such chairs are used in Taoist temples to accommodate the immaterial presence of spirits. They are usually paired with a red-and-gold lacquer tablet that cannot be displayed inside. The main altar of Dat's house is in the same room, but for once there is no statue displayed, the altar being devoted to the ancestors and house spirits. A chest of drawers topped by Buddhist images in various classic poses, liturgical objects in wood or bronze, paintings by Nghiem, and a sitting area filled with beautiful benches and tables carved with stylized Chinese characters create a unique atmosphere.

Dat's office, situated on the third floor, is more modest, but no less elegant. From here there is a wonderful view of the neighboring Quan Su pagoda garden, whose light and trees offer a natural backdrop to the items in his office. His shop offers the same atmosphere of aesthetic grace as his house, this time thanks to the pleasing marriage between the antique furniture and objects and the owner's photographs, many of which feature his daughter with classical musical instruments.

Left The cabinet, placed against an unpainted brick wall, contains an exquisite collection of eleventh-century vases and pots, mostly in brown-glazed terracotta. Most of these pieces where excavated from underground burial sites. Some of the pots recovered still have their original lids.

Below A small altar table with more of Dat's elegant statues is flanked by sets of temple scepters which were used in traditional pagoda ceremonies. These are now collected by dealers in Vietnam. Above the statues on the table hangs an ornately carved panel which would once have stood above an ancestral altar.

斷 能 事 遇

Above Sets of furniture of this type, which includes a table and two benches, were used as a gathering spot in the homes of well-to-do families. They were also used for entertaining guests and for drinking tea, and are now sought after by collectors. Each piece is delicately carved with traditional folk scenes depicting animals and the countryside. The paintings, all of Vietnamese women, represent different periods of twentieth-century Vietnamese art.

Left Dat's office on the third floor looks out onto the garden of the Quan Su Pagoda. His desk is a modern interpretation of a Ming-style piece, a very popular style in modern Vietnamese homes, particularly in the north. A cer-amic garden stand sits on the floor next to Dat's desk.

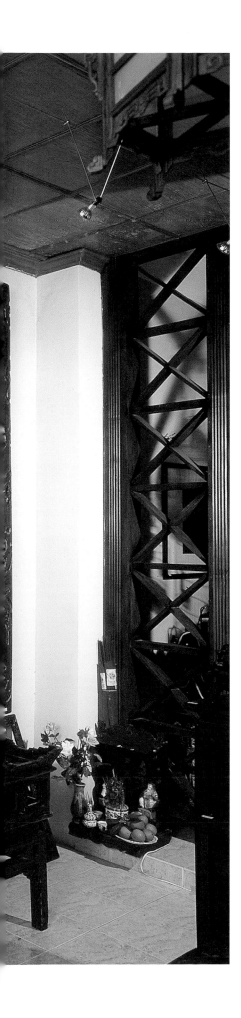

Left A series of photographs by Dat of his daughter alongside traditional Vietnamese instruments are displayed in his shop. On the floor at right is an altar dedicated to the God of Good Fortune, Than Tai. These altars are still used today by most Vietnamese businesses. The main table is a traditional side table used for tea drinking. On top sit various pagoda statues and decorative items.

Above Dat's photographs hang on the walls throughout his shop, many of them depicting scenes from daily life in Vietnam. As in the rest of the house, most of the furniture in the shop is Ming style, reproduced locally by Vietnamese craftsmen.

khanh family home

THE KHANH FAMILY HOME is one of the oldest houses in Ho
Chi Minh City. Built in the 1920s by a rich local banker,
its style is typical of the French colonial houses of the time.
The one-story structure is a classic bungalow designed for
a colonial lifestyle, with overhanging eaves and vertical pillars providing enough exposure to allow balmy breezes and
scented aromas to drift in from the garden. A large frangipani, planted by the original owner, stands grandly guarding
the entrance at the front of the garden, its ancient branches
providing welcome shade over a large area.

Quasar Khanh was born in Hanoi in 1934 and moved
to Paris in 1949 where he made his career as an engineer
and then designer; he is best known for his creation of in-
flatable furniture in the 1960s. He moved back to Vietnam
with his film director son Othello Khanh and designer wife
Michele d'Albert in 1994. To begin with, the family lived
in Hanoi, but soon they moved to Ho Chi Minh City where
Michele began to work with local laquerware artisans and
Quasar developed the world's first bamboo bicycle.

The family completely restored the house, removing all
the false partitioned walls as well as the ceilings so that each
room now opens up to a steep, tiled red roof. The bedrooms
all lead off the large living area where the family congregates
throughout the day and where friends are regularly enter-
tained. The other main structural alteration involved recon-
figuring the back of the house to create an open-plan kitchen
adjoining the living area and bathroom. By restricting the
color scheme to monochrome white walls and black and
white tiles, there is a continuity that runs throughout the
house and into the garden, maximizing the use of the lumi-
nous tropical light.

Once this backdrop was in place, finding furniture and
works of art to fill the space was second nature to the family.
The house is full of items amassed over the years, together
with more contemporary pieces created by this inspiring
team. Khanh's latest collections include aluminum pieces, a
concept he first developed in France: "Aluminum is a light
material and the idea came from less is more." The walls
are adorned with paintings mostly by friends, but a large
family portrait painted by Quasar himself hangs above one
of his aluminum and glass side tables bedecked with photographs, alongside his portrait of Michele (pages 146–7).

Pages 182–3 All of the furniture in the house was either designed and manufactured in Vietnam by Michele and Quasar or brought with them to Vietnam from France when they moved there permanently. A large painting of a reclining lady by the French Vietnamese artist Cong hangs above the piano. The painting on the left, by Quasar, depicts the interior of the Khanh family home in Paris.

Above left The lacquered furniture with aluminum legs in the dining room is designed by both Quasar and Michele. Quasar's now classic standard lamp stands at the far end of the room.

Left Quasar's now classic dining chair in aluminum. Each piece is created using a mold which can only be used once. It is sand-cast and each piece is slightly different.

Above The lacquered bamboo furniture – an occasional table with a glass top, a sofa and armchair, and a sleek black coffee table – was created by Michele. The furniture is very resilient and is equally suitable for outdoors.

Left The table in the dining room is laid with celadon ceramics designed by Michele. A butler's tray from her bamboo furniture collection stands in the corner. A 1930s chrome shelving unit in the kitchen displays an unusual collection of cocktail shakers and glasses.

Right The standard lamp was designed by Quasar and is part of a larger collection of aluminum furniture. Each piece is sand-cast and then polished by hand, the result being that no two pieces are identical.

Below The beams of the high ceiling in the main bedroom are fully exposed, allowing the air to circulate freely. All the fabrics in the room are pale in color which helps to keep the room light and airy. The four-poster bed, with its heavily draped mosquito net, and the furniture and bedside lamp contribute to the overall Indochine feel of the room.

187

Below The marble-topped Long Bar was created by Quasar Khan and was built as a new edition to the bar in 2000. His signature aluminum tubing is used in the shelving and for the legs of the bar stools.

qbar

QBAR WAS OPENED in 1992, and since then it has become a notable part of Ho Chi Minh City's entertainment scene. Its owner and creator, Vietnamese-American Phuong Anh Nguyen, decided on the concept when she returned to her home country in 1992 and observed that the only bars available in the city were located in hotels. She felt it was time her hometown had its own modern bar.

Situated underneath one of Phuong Anh's favorite buildings, the old French-built Opera House between the Caravelle and Continental hotels, QBar is the perfect site for a bar. The building itself has been transformed a number of times; during the 1950s it briefly became the House of Representative and it did not revert to its original usage until the early 1990s.

Characteriscally, Phuong Anh dispensed with interior designers as far as possible and fashioned the bar in her own style. All the furniture was produced locally, and she employed local artists to create the atmosphere she envisioned. "Given our location, I wanted to create a theatrical neoclassical feel, a place that is entirely comfortable, with plenty to look at so you never want to leave."

This translated into gilded ceilings, marbled columns and rococo-styled furniture. Large extravagantly styled gilded doorways divide seating areas and cleverly frame the Caravaggio-inspired paintings on the wall either side of the main bar area. Lighting plays an important part, with crystal beads attached to tube piping made by Phuong Anh hanging in the Silver Bar, and Fortuny-inspired silk chandeliers painted by the same artist who created the rococo-style wall paintings.

Phuong Anh also used perspex and glass panels to great effect, playing with photographic sheets of color which can be changed to create different moods. On another wall hangs a perspex lightbox framing a gold candelabra – a piece of art in itself. Perspex is also innovatively used in the tables created by friend Andrew Currie, which catch the light and reflect the images of the chandeliers above.

The architecture of this classic building guides your eye. A series of original archways leads to different bar areas, each with its own ambience. The Long Bar, created by designer Quasar Khanh, is located in the basement of the old Opera House, with old storage spaces serving as natural alcoves for seating. Through another archway, plump red leather banquettes and purple lacquered-topped tables gather by the Copper Bar. Look further up on to the street either side of the building and identical fountains stand proudly flanking this great city landmark.

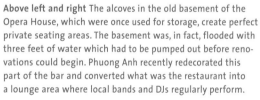

Above left and right The alcoves in the old basement of the Opera House, which were once used for storage, create perfect private seating areas. The basement was, in fact, flooded with three feet of water which had to be pumped out before renovations could begin. Phuong Anh recently redecorated this part of the bar and converted what was the restaurant into a lounge area where local bands and DJs regularly perform.

Right Fortuny-inspired silk chandeliers hang above a painted passageway leading to the Copper Bar. This is where Phuong Anh's husband, Sean Mulraine, prefers to be as he greets and watches over the city's élite.

Opposite Red leather upholstered banquettes in the lounge bar sit either side of the gold rococo-style double doorway, which forms a novel frame for the Caravaggio-inspired wall paintings.

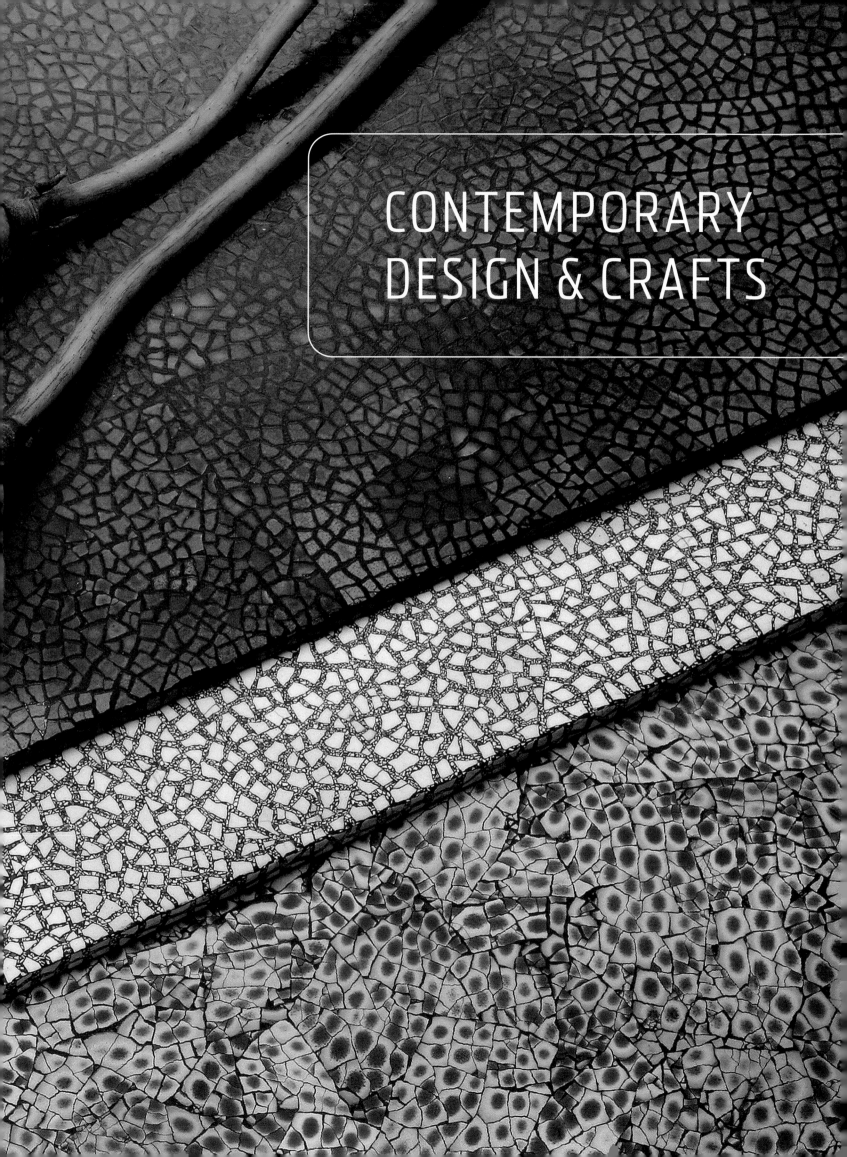

CONTEMPORARY DESIGN & CRAFTS

furniture

Pages 192–3 This rectangular table is lacquered using crushed eggshell, which gives it a light color. This technique was popularized by Jean Durand at the beginning of the twentieth century.

Below left A ying/yang sofa set is displayed in Gaya alongside tall rattan light shades and a large bamboo screen, all designed and manufactured by Lawson Johnston.

Bottom left The Alfie lounger is made of aluminum and woven poly rattan which, unlike more traditional fabrics, can be left outside in all weathers. These products are now being used by hotels all over Asia.

Below The Louis armchair is a comfortable egg-shaped seat made out of wicker. The cushions are in leather. The moon light hanging above is by Catherine Denoual.

THE WATER HYACINTH was thought to have been introduced into Asia by European explorers some time during the nineteenth century. It was widely distributed because of the beauty of its large purple flowers and upright green leaves, which act as sails floating along the rivers of the Mekong delta. However, it is also regarded by most scientists as one of the world's most noxious aquatic weeds, and in Vietnam, as in other Southeast Asian countries, it has come to be regarded as an economic opportunity. The plant is harvested and cleaned and then dried in the sun to ensure that it retains a natural bleached color. It is then processed into a variety of exotic products, including furniture and baskets. These types of products have only been in production for a few years in Vietnam but they are rapidly gaining the attention of designers from around the world for their unique appearance and durability.

Lawson Johnston was the first person to manufacture water hyacinth furniture and other types of household products in Vietnam. His naturally chic retro modern pieces exude a simple yet opulent style. Oversized sofas with linen covers create the perfect relaxed, laid-back atmosphere in a tropical climate. Water hyancinth is naturally soft in texture, but also masculine. Many of his designs are bought by designers all over the world, and he has been involved in the decoration of a number of resort projects in Vietnam.

Left A large hanging pod chair created by Lawson Johnston hangs in the garden of his house. The chair is made of woven rattan, which is an extremely tough and durable material.

Below The Assheton armchair was created by Lawson for the Foreign Correspondents Club in Siem Reap. The chest of drawers behind is silver gilded and displays a collection of thirteenth-century ceramics.

Bottom The large checkered weave water hyacinth sofas were one of Lawson's early designs. Hanging on the wall behind the sofa is a topographical map of southern Vietnam from the 1950s. A matching map of northern Vietnam hangs on the main staircase in the hall of Lawson's house.

baskets

WATER HYACINTH, rattan, palm leaves and other natural products are all commonly woven into items such as baskets, boxes, mats and other types of everyday household items. Indeed, weaving is one of the oldest crafts in Vietnam and woven products are ubiquitous throughout the country. The materials used are generally extremely strong and durable even though in some cases the products themselves may appear fragile. Today, more modern shapes and designs are being created and are often combined with other materials such as leather or wood. And whereas traditionally woven products were left in their natural state, today they are just as likely to be dyed or stained to suit more contemporary tastes. Some shapes still tend to be fairly simple, with a subtle elegant movement in the fabric. Other, more durable, products may be constructed using either a bamboo or metal framework, and in some cases can be quite structured. In Western as well as traditional Vietnamese homes, these types of woven products would traditionally have only been used for their original purpose, whereas today they just as likely to be used as part of the aesthetics of an interior.

Below Water hyacinth baskets with leather handles are ideal for shopping or a trip to the beach.

Right, clockwise from top These laundry baskets and containers, also made from water hyacinth, have been reinforced with a bamboo frame for extra strength.

Compartmentalized water hyacinth boxes provide useful storage.

Both these rattan boxes and the water hyacinth baskets at right make useful storage spaces in any house or apartment. They are attractive and hard-wearing.

Bamboo is extremely versatile and probably the strongest of all the natural fibers used in weaving. This set of baskets has been created for use in the kitchen and includes bowls, trays and a bottle holder.

Triple-weave water hyacinth can be hand-dyed, as shown here, or left a natural color.

lights

Below These lights, placed on the floor and on an eggshell lacquered plinth, are aesthetic rather than practical, each being a beautiful object in itself. A range of natural materials have been used in their manufacture, including resin, bamboo and silk.

Right These lights, artfully arranged on a shelving unit, appear to glow and are perfect in the corner of a room or on a low table drawing your eye subtly in. They are ideal for setting the mood in a room.

LIGHTING plays an important part in Vietnamese contemporary design. Lights are an integral part of a room's furniture and an essential element in creating the right kind of atmosphere.

Modern lighting of the type shown here provides a soft, warm light that is both very flattering and comforting. Made from a range of materials, including rattan, bamboo, wood, rice paper, silk, shell, resin, metal and lacquer, these soothing lights are appropriate for the end of a long day. The effect of the materials used in a design can be very different. Some materials used can result in a more rustic, traditional-looking product, such as a lightshade sculptured in bamboo on a wooden stand. Other materials, such as resin or lacquer, may result in a more cosmopolitan look.

Color is important as it often determines the mood and the style of a room. Lights come in a range of shades, mimicking either the coolness of natural daylight or warmer, candlelight tones. They mimic traditional domestic shapes and styles and are turned into more modern structured objects. Different lights can be used in different parts of a room – on a table or desk, on the floor in the corner of a room, or simply put on a plinth or a shelf.

embroidery

THE SEVENTEENTH-CENTURY craftsman Le Cong Hanh is often considered to be the creator of Vietnamese embroidering. He combined Chinese techniques with those of the Vietnamese to create a new, artistic form. By the early twentieth century, Vietnamese artisans were admired for their embroidered masterpieces specially created for the royal court, although sadly very few of these original pieces remain.

Vietnamese embroidery is currently enjoying a resurgence, and is being employed by local and international designers on products ranging from flags and banners to handbags and clothes. French fashion designer Valerie Gregori McKenzie, who has lived in Vietnam for the past fifteen years, was one of the first to apply these ancient skills to contemporary designs. Over the years, she has built up a dedicated local team skilled in the art of embroidery. The workers, mostly married women living in villages around Hanoi, spend much of their time in the paddy fields, particularly around harvest time, but during off-peak periods and seasons can earn additional income embroidering at home.

Inspired by the exceptional hand work she found, Valerie began producing a collection of textiles based on intricately embroidered designs applied to luxury fabrics such as velvets, linens, hand-dyed silks and unbleached cottons. Her velvet and silk cushions, in dramatic colors such as Chinese red or duck egg blue, have a lovingly worked embroidered pattern and are sometimes finished with a separate binding or button. Not only do they form a decorative impact through the juxtaposition of colors and textures, but they create a natural bridge between interiors and fashion.

Below Valerie uses silks and velvets in contrasting shades, giving these cushions a structured look.

Bottom Folk design cushions decorate a daybed at the Evason Hideaway resort (page 166).

Right All these cushions have different textures and are pilled together effectively across a hand-embroided silk throw.

Below right The intricate embroidery on this throw and these cushions can take one person up to a month to complete.

lacquerware

VIETNAMESE ARTISANS have been producing lacquer for centuries. Lacquerware, along with celadon, can perhaps be considered the country's most significant contribution to the world of fine art. In northern Vietnam, the tradition of harvesting lacquer dates back more than twenty centuries. It is here that the early Vietnamese artisans discovered how to use the liquid derived from the *Rhus succedanea* tree and convert it into a slow-drying natural lacquer to decorate delicate objects and other forms of art. The process is complicated. Traditionally, Vietnamese lacquer-making techniques require at least twelve layers of lacquer. Each layer is dried and then polished with water before a new layer of lacquer is applied. A simple surface takes a minimum of two months to create.

At the beginning of the twentieth century, Art Deco artists such as the Frenchman Jean Dunand used lacquer from Vietnam to combine age-old techniques with contempory forms and designs to create pieces that exemplified the sophisticated tastes of the time. Dunand employed hundreds of craftsmen and assistants, including a number of Indo-Chinese lacquer workers. His eggshell lacquer became so popular that he kept chickens in the yard of his workshop. Today, Michele d'Albert is among a number of designers producing contemporary pieces. When Michele first started working with Vietnamese lacquerware artists, they were highly skilled but would only produce the traditional dark red and black lacquers. She introduced bright colors to everyday objects by adding new pigments to traditional lacquer mixes.

Below and right Vietnamese artisans have been producing lacquerware for centuries, especially the traditional dark red and black lacquer wares. More recently, French designer Michele d'Albert has given lacquer a fresh new twist. Capitalizing on the skills of artisans, she has adapted ancient techniques to produce exciting new shapes and introduced bright colors by adding new pigments to traditional lacquer mixes. Her designs are inspired by traditional Asian shapes and ideas but she has successfully bridged the gap between age-old techniques and contemporary needs.

ceramics

By the fifteenth century, some of the most interesting ceramics in Asia were being produced not in China but in the north of Vietnam, particularly blue-and-white ceramics. Trade was flourishing and the result was a burst of creativity that is reflected in today's modern designs.

An extensive and diverse range of shapes and designs are now being produced. Most are skillfully but routinely manufactured items, often reflecting the trade ceramics produced in the past. These include underglaze blue-decorated wares embellished with fine examples of Vietnamese ceramic painters' art. Patterns range from mythical animals such as dragons and fish to exotic foliage with flowering trees or lush plants. Many of these modern pieces are almost indistinguishable to the naked eye from the finest antique examples.

Celadon ware has an even longer history in Vietnam, with early examples dating back to the sixth century. Over the centuries, the techniques have been perfected. Vietnamese celadon is distinguished by its simple yet refined shapes and its almost jade-like glaze, although firing inconsistencies are common. Celadon clay has to come from the north of Vietnam. It is most famously produced in Ba Trang village outside Hanoi, where the same families have been producing celadon for generations using closely guarded glazing recipes. A celadon glaze is mixed with a metallic pigment which comes out a gray color before it is fired. This makes the color very difficult to judge as the results only appear after the product has been fired.

Below Celadon Green, owned by Michele d'Albert, produces both functional and decorative items.

Right, clockwise from top Modern-day celadon designs are often inspired by fifteenth-century designs, which were made in Chinese-run factories in northern Vietnam.

Black and white ceramics of varying sizes and shapes are grouped in an informal display.

A contemporary underglaze blue and enamel fish plate follows fifteenth-century techniques.

Sleek ceramics by local firm Emu include matt black (and white) ceramic tea or coffee sets.

A blue-and-white bowl and celadon plate mix traditional elegance with practicality, functionality and form.

propaganda art

THE WORD "PROPAGANDA" more often that not evokes negative connotations. Formal interpretations describe it as a planned use of information that is spread for the purpose of promoting some type of cause. One of the most provocative forms of propaganda is art although literature and the cinema are other mediums. In Vietnam, it was President Ho Chi Minh who recognized the potential of the power of political messages through art, and by the mid-1950s propaganda art was being used as a powerful tool of communication.

It was used mainly to motivate and inspire the Vietnamese people who were fighting for independence and later reunification of their country in what later became known in Vietnam as the American War. Posters of that time reflect an entire society focused on the national fight to liberate the south and unify the country. Not surprisingly, the work was not always seen as art, but more as a conduit of public information. Posters were exhibited all over the country with the aim of spreading messages to as many people as possible.

Propaganda artists combined traditional and contemporary techniques using a diverse range of media, including hand-painted posters, paintings on rice paper, watercolors and pen-and-ink sketches. A poster would typically contain a color image with a short message such as "The fire of struggle is roaring" or, more pertinently, "The world must have peace." Many themes were used but often the same ones would reappear with great regularity.

There is a small downtown boutique in Ho Chi Minh City called Saigon Kitsch, which has taken some of these original designs and produced a range of products that would look electric on any table. The company has produced glassware and table mats, mugs and posters, all faithfully following the designs of the original artists. Upstairs, in the Art Gallery Dogma, many of the original posters are exhibited for the first time since the 1950s. A small window is thus opening on this long-forgotten period of twentieth-century Vietnamese art.

Pages 206–7 A variety of propaganda images inspired by the American War, reproduced on table mats, coasters, glasses and mugs by Saigon Kitsch, a small downtown boutique in Ho Chi Minh City. The poster on page 206 reads "Industrialization – Modernization for the happiness of people."

acknowledgments

The authors and photographer are grateful to the following people for their assistance during the process of researching, photographing and writing this book:

An Khanh, Lee Baker, Michael Baron, Clair Burket, Mrs Cuc and Mr Hoa, Michele d'Albert, Jenny Degussa, Loan de Leo Foster, Catherine Denoual, Diep Dong family, Do Mong Thuy, Doan Dai Tu, director and staff of the Vietnam Museum of Ethnology, director of the Ford Foundation, Le Phuc, Lucy Forwood, Richard Forwood, Valerie Gregori McKenzie, T. J. Grundle-hong of Evason Hideaway, The Hideaway Café, Mrs Hien, Lawson Johnston, Psyche Kennet, Khanh Minh Tran, Othello Khanh, Quasar Khanh, Suzanne Lecht, Luc Lejeune, Sean Mulraine, Nguyen Van Hung, Phuong An Nguyen, Julia Richards, Arache Sarai and staff at Gaya, Dominic Scriven, Stella So, manager and staff of the Sofitel Metropole Hanoi, Mr Son and staff of the Emperor Restaurant, Rene Tayeb, Thai Thai, Tran family, Tran Manh Dat.

Among the above are home-owners and residents who warmly welcomed us into their homes despite the inevitable inconvenience.

Special thanks go to Julia Richards from the Chesterton Petty Company, designer Valerie Gregori McKenzie and Le Phuc, General Secretary of the Vietnamese Photographers' Association, whose help was so decisive at the start of this project.

The staff of the Hue citadel and mausoleums, as well as the monks and caretakers of several temples and pagodas in Vietnam, especially in Hoa Lu and Chua Keo, also deserve a special mention for allowing us to photograph these places.

This book would also not have been possible without the support of the City and Province People's Committees and their staff in Hanoi, Hue, Ho Chi Minh City and Phu Quoc, who were invariably supportive and took a special interest in the project.

Co-author Bertrand Hartingh is also indebted to Professor Ha Van Tan, whose book on *Vietnam Dinhs*, co-authored with Nguyen Van, is the only detailed work about these magnificent buildings, and to Roxana Waterson, whose work, *The Living House: An Anthropology of Architecture in South-East Asia*, is a must for anyone interested in Southeast Asian cultures.

Thanks also go to all the designers, shops and galleries whose work is featured in the book and to the recreation outlets who allowed on-site photography.

Appeal Shop
(Contact: Stella So)
41 Ton That Thiep Street, District 1, Ho Chi Minh City
tel: (84 8) 821 3614; e-mail: gta@hcmc.netnam.vn

Art Vietnam Gallery
(Contact: Suzanne Lecht)
30 Hang Than Street, Hanoi
tel: (84 4) 927 2349; fax: (84 4) 927 2804; e-mail: artvietnamgallery@gmail.com

Catherine Denoual Maison
15c Thi Sach Street, District 1, Ho Chi Minh City
tel: (84 8) 823 9394; e-mail: cath@catherinedenoual.com

Celadon Green
(Contact: Michele d'Albert)
6/39A Tran Nao, Street 12, District 2, Ho Chi Minh City
tel: (84 8) 914 4697

Dogma
1st floor, 43 Ton That Thiep Street, District 1, Ho Chi Minh City
tel: (84 8) 825 6817

Emu
43 Ton That Thiep Street, District 1, Ho Chi Minh City
tel: (84 8) 914 3345; fax: (84 8) 914 3346; e-mail: info@emuvietnam.com

Evason Hideaway
Beachside Tran Phu, Nha Trang
tel: (058) 522 222; fax: (058) 525 858; e-mail: reservations-anamandara@evasonresorts.com

Gaya
(Contact: Arache Sarai)
39 Ton That Thiep District 1, Ho Chi Minh City
tel: (84 8) 744 4713; fax: (84 8) 744 4905; e-mail: gayavietnam@hcm.vnn.vn

Mekong Merchant
(Contact: Ms Vuong My Linh)
23 Thao Dien Street, An Phu District 2, Ho Chi Minh City
tel: (84 8) 744 4713; fax: (84 8) 744 4905; e-mail: info@mekongmerchant.com

Quasar Khanh International
(Contact: Michele d'Albert)
6/39A Tran Nao, Street 12, District 2, Ho Chi Minh City
tel: (84 8) 740 4033; fax: (84 8) 740 4032; e-mail: quasarkhanh@hcm.vnn.vn

Qbar
Opera House, 7 Lam Son Square, District 1, Ho Chi Minh City
tel: (84 8) 823 3479

Saigon Kitsch
43 Ton That Thiep Street, Distict 1, Ho Chi Minh City
tel: (84 8) 821 8019; fax: (84 8) 914 3346; e-mail: info@saigonkitsch.com

Song
(Contact: Valery Gregori McKenzie)
47 Ky Con Street, District 1, Ho Chi Minh City
tel: (84 8) 914 4088; fax: (84 8) 914 4089; e-mail: sales@asiasongdesign.com

Spa Tropic
(Contact: Do Mong Thuy)
187B Hai Ba Trung Street, District 3, Ho Chi Minh City
tel: (84 8) 822 8895; fax: (84 8) 822 8895; e-mail: info@spatropic.com

Temple Club
29 Ton That Thiep Street, District 1, Ho Chi Minh City
tel: (84 8) 829 9244; fax: (84 8) 914 4271; e-mail: templeclub@hcm.vnn.vn